The Art of Cidermaking

By Paul Correnty

Brewers Publications, Boulder, Colorado

The Art of Cidermaking
Copy Editors: Celeste Clingan and Bill Simpson
Technical Editor: Gabriel Ostriker
Copyright © 1995 by Paul Correnty

ISBN 0-937381-42-X
Printed in the United States of America
10 9 8 7 6 5 4 3 2 1

Written by Paul Correnty

Cover Design: Marilyn Cohen
Cover Photography: Galen Nathanson
Interior Design: Marilyn Cohen and Wendy Rodgers
Interior Photography: Elizabeth Gold, Charlie Olchowski, and Don Pugh
Interior Illustrations: Greg Dye
Thanks to the Niwot Antique Emporium for the oak barrel used in cover photo.
Published by Brewers Publications Inc., USA, a division of the Association of
Brewers Inc., PO Box 1679, Boulder, CO 80306-1679, USA; (303) 447-0816,
FAX (303) 447-2825.

Direct all inquires/orders to the above address. All rights reserved. Except
for use in review, no portion of this book may be reproduced in any form
without the written permission of the publisher. Neither the authors, editors,
nor the publisher assumes any responsibility for the use or misuse of information contained in this book.

Table of Contents

About the Author

I got my first taste of fermented cider while in France as a teenager, having moved there from Florida with my family. As a matter of fact, I got my first taste of a lot of things there, but this book is about cider so I'll stick to the subject.

After graduating with a baccalaureate in economics from a Jesuit-run French school, I set out to see the world and wound up in San Francisco. It was the Napa and Sonoma wine country that really got me interested in fermented beverages, but before I could pursue any further interest in wine I headed to Massachusetts to help open a restaurant with other family members.

Harsh winters are not kind to wine-producing grapes, but New England has no peers in North America as far as apples are concerned. Imagine my surprise to find out that almost none of these beauties

were being turned into fermented cider. What a waste of perfectly good apples! At my wife's urging, I managed to glean a few tidbits of information from some of the old farmers who always put up a barrel or two for the winter, and we made our first batch more than ten years ago.

Since that time I've done everything I could to convince people that it is their patriotic duty to make hard cider. Articles in **Zymurgy**® (the journal of the American Homebrewers Association®), cidermaking classes and demonstrations, as well as the annual fall CiderFest in Westford, Massachusetts, have all contributed to this country's awakening to America's classic beverage.

I currently reside in Pepperell, Massachusetts, with my wife, Anita, and son, Fritz. Sharing our 200-year old residence are a couple of cats, a family of bats, and various critters.

Acknowledgements

Without a doubt, HUGE thanks go to Brewers Publications publisher Elizabeth Gold. Faced with my constant delays, her Job-like patience and the professionalism of her staff are really what carried this book to print. A large tankard of cider for you all.

Harriet Hornblower contributed much of the historical background of cider and researched the very beginnings of apple cultivation. This detective work meant long hours poring over old texts written in a variety of languages. For adding the necessary information and coming through in a pinch, I owe my friend Harriet an enormous thank you and unlimited raspberry cider, whether we dine on Alaskan smoked salmon or not.

To the home-brewers of this country: I am indebted to you for reviving the art of making fermented cider and proudly pro-moting it alongside real ale. Members of the Boston Wort Processors homebrew club in particular have been instrumental in helping restore hard cider to its rightful place in our homes and taverns.

A tip o' the jug to the Yankee farmers of New England. For decades they were the keepers of the craft until the homebrewers became enlightened (or did they just need something to do in between brewing Oktoberfest and holiday ales?).

A kiss to my sweetheart Anita for all her encouragement through the many apple harvests. A grateful thanks for the chapters of text you rescued from crash land and for showing me how to back up files on diskette.

Finally, with the greatest love and appreciation, I thank my parents Mémé and Vieux. They had the courage to risk everything so their kids could experience a way of life most could only dream about. I dedicate this book to you both, for without the move, who knows what awful soda I'd be drinking now.

Introduction

A piece of the apple pie was missing. In 1980, when I gazed upon acres and acres of New England's magnificent old orchards, I realized something was lacking. Thirty or more varieties of apples were for sale during the season. One could purchase apple butter, apple sauce, mile-high apple pie, candied apples, baked apples, dried apples, and even fresh pressed sweet apple cider. But where was the highest form of appledom, the pinnacle of what is apple, the exquisite result of the process between yeast and juice? Alas, throughout the land hard cider was nowhere to be found.

How could that be? What had led to the demise of the American cider tradition? After surviving and thriving for centuries, had hard cider finally lost its appeal? I couldn't believe that was the case. After all, hard cider, in one form or another, has outlasted numerous cultures, empires, and prohibition drives. For centuries, it had thrived in Rome, Greece, Renaissance Europe, and Colonial America. It crossed the lines of religions, politics, and social classes. I found it impossible to believe that such a drink could be left to the annals of history. So with the thirst I had acquired for this beverage while traveling in England and France, I set out with two goals in mind:

• find the old-timers who still practiced this craft and learn the traditional methods and principles of making hard cider.
• revive the proud, but long-forgotten, 300-year-old tradition of cidermaking in America.

Fortunately, my quest led to a group previously unknown to me: the American Homebrewers Association®, whose efforts to revive real beer matched my own attempts as far as fermented cider was concerned. A few draughts of hard cider was all it took to convince these brewers that I was giving them the straight scoop. Cider tastes too good and is too easy to make to be cast into the dustbin of beverage history.

Therefore, be a cider patriot and discover how to make and enjoy yesterday's revolutionary beverage with today's modern methods. Making terrific cider is easy, now ridiculously so with the boom in fully stocked, 1-800 homebrew supply stores and the availability of fresh-pressed sweet cider in the fall. So get out into the orchards and rediscover this traditional beverage.

What Cider Is

The term cider has various meanings, all of which add to the confusion of defining it. In the United States, cider can mean either the unfermented, non-alcoholic drink commonly referred to as sweet cider or it can mean the yeast-fermented, alcohol-containing beverage called hard cider. In Great Britain, however, cider is only an alcoholic beverage made from fermented apple juice, so the term hard cider is redundant.

Making cider is simple, so why should defining it be so complicated? Since this book deals primarily with the yeast-fermented, alcohol-containing drink, we will refer to the fermented beverage as cider or hard cider. The unfermented non-alcoholic juice from the pressed apples will be referred to simply as sweet cider.

Above all, hard cider is a fantastic beverage, wonderfully aromatic and flavorful with a reminder of autumn in every draught.

For practical purposes, cider that goes beyond 14 percent alcohol by volume (11 percent alcohol by weight) — referred to as rocket fuel, liquid death, brain scrambler, or any one of many terms used to designate a beverage used solely for its intoxicating abilities — is of no use to the home cidermaker.

Cidermakers actively promote the craft by practicing what they do, which is making a healthy and natural beverage that can be part of a healthy and responsible lifestyle. In this effort, cidermakers are joined by their brethren, homebrewers and winemakers. Making a high-alcohol cider diminishes the taste of the finished product. A cider too high in alcohol is harsh and unpleasant to drink. Even though cider can be almost any fermented apple beverage, cider that is truly worthy of its name is made with care and attention. With a minimum of effort, equipment, and expertise, you too can quickly become a cidermaker and a damn good one at that.

Why Make Cider?

There are as many reasons for making your own fermented cider as there are apples on a tree. One reason is the lack of commercial hard cider available is the United States, unlike the situation in Europe or Canada. The available American ciders are produced by small cideries or microbreweries and, although high in quality, they are only distributed for a local or regional market. The handful of imports (especially from the United Kingdom) are produced by giant conglomerates and, as a whole, are not very interesting. The best way to prevent a bottleneck of supplies and a shortage of cider is to have plenty of full bottlenecks down in the cellar.

The home cidermaker is able

APPLES HEADED FOR THE CONVEYOR AT PINE HILL ORCHARDS, COLRAIN, MASS.

PHOTO BY: CHARLIE OLCHOWSKI AND DON PUGH

to take the world by the apples and proclaim, "To hell with standardization! I want something with gusto, something distinctive!" Your imagination and good taste can be your guide, because hard cider blends well with many different fruits, spices, and sweeteners. And you know your finished cider will meet the highest quality standards because you are in control of what goes into your cider and what stays out.

Making cider is not only easy, it's ridiculously easy. No boiling, no straining, no pressing, no sweat. Plus, the cidermaking ingredients and supplies are relatively inexpensive. Maybe the question should be "Why not make cider?" The satisfaction of making your own superb cider with a minimum of fuss and expense while carrying on a great American tradition is just too good a deal to pass up.

How This Book Is Set Up

This book has three distinct sections to guide you along on your cidermaking journey. Part one, "History," covers the development of cider as we know it today. After a look at cider's past, you will be craving a taste of this time-tested beverage.

Part two, "First Timers," outlines the art of making cider at home. The information is designed for the inquisitive newcomer, with or without homebrewing or winemaking experience, to the world of homemade ciders. This section explains the procedures for turning sweet, unfermented apple cider into hard cider, and includes information on the equipment you'll need, sanitation procedures, sweet cider composition and where to buy it, and bottling your finished hard cider. Everything you need to make your first batch a bubbling success is included.

Part three, "Seasoned Pros," is for experienced brewers, winemakers, and/or cidermakers. This section details the art of blending juices from different apple varieties, custom pressing your own apples, choosing the proper yeast strains, and oak aging and caring for your oak casks. This section also includes a chapter of special cider recipes. Whether you follow them exactly or modify them to your seasoned palate, you won't be disappointed either way. "Seasoned Pros" ends with guidelines for judging and evaluating cider, complete with a discussion of cider components, a cider score sheet, and a list of the different cider categories.

The Old World

To look at a drink as timeless and beautiful as hard cider without knowing something about the history of the fruit and its early development into cider would be like looking at a fine painting without any knowledge of the artist or the era during which the work was created. Hard cider is a masterpiece that carries the flavor of the fruit, while continuously adjusting to the tastes of culture and the cidermaker.

MYTH AND RELIGION

Part of the reason hard cider has spanned centuries and cultures is the connections both the drink and the apple have to myths and religions (that and its great taste of course). Mythology, wicca craft, Catholicism, and virtually every religion in between have some belief or tradition that incorporates the apple or its fermented counterpart, cider.

Before we go into any specific ties, let's first demonstrate why the apple may play a part in so many of these myths and religions.

Go into your kitchen and grab a nice, ripe apple and a sharp knife. Don't worry, this isn't any kind of sacrificial ceremony. Cut the apple through the middle, halfway between the stem and the base. Notice the pattern the seeds form in the loci (the five leathery seed chambers) and the five-pointed star, or pentacle, created from the cross-section of the stem. The five-pointed star has a long-standing "occult" or hidden meaning in the mythical traditions of Europe. This star is the mystic symbol of protection and perfection. It is one of the more profound signs in magic when placed inside a circle with its five points touching the circumference. Like the five-pointed star, the apple is both the symbol for valor and deceit. This paradox at the core of the apple, forgive the pun, is also the paradox of the apple's legacy in myth and religion.

According to some interpretations of the Bible, the apple played a key role in humanity's development. But most of those interpretations give the apple the unfortunate role as the tool for the fall of humanity from the grace of God. The supposed location of the Garden of Eden makes it doubtful, however, that apples would have even been present because they need cooler climates to thrive.

In many pagan cultures of early Europe, the apple was a mystical staple. With the apple, poets and bards could supposedly access the divine, speak to the dead, and communicate with the spirits of the crops and the seasons. In many of these cultures, the apple tree and its fruit were regarded as sacred to the point that cutting down an apple tree was often punishable by death.

Even the English custom known as Christmas caroling has ties to these pagan traditions. The carol was a salute to the trees that, come spring, would produce apples for cider. English farmers maintained the midwinter custom of wassailing their fruit orchards the night before Christmas eve. Wassail is a midwinter punch made with cider, spices, and baked apples. Each of the fruit-growing counties in England celebrated this custom differently. The villagers of Kent, Devon, Somerset, and Gloucestershire would descend on the household that had prepared the bowl of wassail. The group would grab the bowl and troop off to the orchard and place the wassail down by the largest apple tree. Then, each person would ladle up a large cup of wassail, drink what they could, and throw whatever remained on the tree roots. In one town, pieces of toast soaked in cider were hung on the tree to appeal to the tree spirits. In the orchards of several communities, the people hit the trunks of the apple trees with sticks and sang songs to encourage the trees to bear a fine yield.

EARLY HISTORY

Aside from the mythical aspect, much scientific research has been conducted to investigate the apple's history. Pinpointing the first apple or the first glass of cider is as impossible as pinpointing the first blade of grass. The apple's existence is believed to be at least as old as the earliest records of

mankind. Ethnobotanists believe that depictions of wild apples appear in Paleolithic cave art dating from between 35,000 and 8,000 B.C. The earliest wild apple species were found in a wide, temperate zone from Asia Minor across the central Asian steppes and into present day India and Pakistan. Archaeologists have also discovered the carbonized remains of wild apples preserved in Neolithic Swiss and Italian lake dwelling sites dating from 2,000 to 1,600 B.C., according to *Smithsonian Timelines of the Ancient World* by Chris Scarre (Dorling Kindersley, 1993). Early documents and archaeological findings reveal that apple propagation began in Europe more than 2,000 years ago. Records from Bronze-Age civilizations flourishing around the Mediterranean shores mention the use of the Sidonian apple (actually they were quinces) in their cuisine. Apple seeds — most likely from Sidonia — have also been discovered in burial offerings in the Egyptian pyramids. By 4 B.C., the Greeks were growing a variety of true apples, most likely on the cool slopes of Macedonia.

These early apple cultivators must have realized that apples are not "true genetic breeders." This means that propagation by seed does not produce as fine a tree as the parent. The only way to ensure reproduction of a particular tree is to graft part of it onto the root stock of another apple tree. Creating a desirable apple may have been as easy as finding a good tree to graft or as difficult as putting together a jig-saw puzzle without any idea of what the finished product should look like. Many of the wild apple varieties were probably small and sour, more like crab apples than nice Red Delicious or McIntosh. Ethnobotanists currently believe that as many as seven different strands of apples contributed genetically to the strand that was eventually cultivated.

The path from cultivated apple to cider is a bit convoluted, but the most likely scenario that led to large-scale production of cider in France and England began with the Moors. The cultivated apple best suited for cidermaking was most likely developed by

the Arab Moors during their occupation of
what is now Spain. The Arabs had translated
the classical texts of the early Romans and
Greeks, including Pilny's *Historia Naturalis*
and Marcus Portius Cato's *De Agricultura*.
These works contained the essential information about the science of growing. When the
European Christians conquered the Moors,
they translated the Arabic texts and took the
new information, along with several late-
ripening apples developed by the Moors. In
Normandy, France, the European milling and
processing technology, developed primarily
for extracting the oil from olives, was combined with the new agricultural information,
and a European cider enterprise was born.

The enterprise was limited, however,
because cider failed to compete with wine in
most of France. Cider at this time was actually more like an apple wine than today's cider:
it was made with the fermented juice from
the strong first pressing of apples. In this
form, the beverage was expensive and only
available to the upper class, but the upper
class preferred wine. In approximately the
sixteenth century, water was added to this
apple wine and later pressings of the apples
were used, making it more available to the
common person. That's when cider's popularity took off. From the sixteenth to the eigh-
teenth centuries, cider was the drink of the
common man, even becoming part of servant
and laborer wages. It was servants and laborers who brought their taste for cider with
them on their voyage across the Atlantic to
the New World.

CHAPTER 2

The New World

Colonists to the New World brought with them the foods, crafts, and customs of their homelands. The English and French settlers in particular were familiar with cider, and their love of this fermented juice meshed perfectly with their new environment. Because the growing conditions were favorable in New England, it was inevitable that "... as the orchards were planted and came to maturity, cider, the native wine of New England, became a common beverage," according to Abiel Livermoor in *History of Wilton, New Hampshire, 1762-1888.*

The thin, rocky soil of New England, so poor for grains and other crops, was ideal for the cultivation of certain tree fruit, especially apples and pears. John Palfrey of Wilton, New Hampshire, wrote that "the apple-tree, set out in extensive orchards, soon produced a fruit far superior in size and flavour to what it had borne on English ground." It didn't take long for new varieties to develop. By 1647, the Roxbury Russet was first identified in an orchard on the hills of Roxbury outside of Boston. This variety is still cultivated and has kept its 300-year-old reputation as the finest North American cider apple.

Hundreds of new varieties spilled forth from the extensive orchards, and thousands upon thousands of gallons of hard cider were produced on the farms of this agricultural land. The figures are staggering according to Vrest Orton's *The American Cider Book* (Farrar, Straus and Giroux, 1973): in 1721 a single village of forty families produced more than 3,000 barrels of cider. In 1767, it was reported that the per capita consumption of cider in Massachusetts was 1.14 barrels!

COLONIAL CULTURE

The spread of apples througout young America was probably the result of two factors: (1) cider was a drink for everyone: school children, servants, ladies, laborers, and even the elite, and (2) a man named John Chapman. Virtually everyone drank cider. It was served to college students, field hands, and slaves. It was deemed suitable for children and ladies as well as for men like our Founding Fathers. President John Adams was fond of a tankard of cider every morning upon arising – and he lived to be 91 years old!

After the American Revolution, a man named John Chapman became one of America's first folk heroes. Chapman, also known as Johnny Appleseed, traveled the developing frontier with a sack of apple seeds over his shoulder. "His mission in life was to see that every farm in the midwest had an orchard," according to Elizabeth Helfman's *Apples, Apples, Apples* (T. Nelson, 1977). Purchasing land with apple seedlings, Chapman eventually accumulated 1,200 acres of land, which he turned into apple nurseries whenever he could.

Hard cider was even used as a political tool, not only to quench the thirsts of people gathered at political meetings and keep them in good spirits, but also to display that a candidate was "of the people." The best example of this is the bitter presidential campaign of 1840.

The Democrats had nominated the incumbent Martin Van Buren as their candidate, and the Whigs countered by nominating General William Harrison. The differences between the two candidates were clear. Van Buren was perceived as a cosmopolitan, far removed from the rough and tumble backwoods of the growing country and overly concerned with his looks. General Harrison, on the other hand, was a true man of the frontier, rising through the military to become a hero by leading troops against the Shawnee chief Tecumseh in 1811 at the village of Tippecanoe. The phrase "Tippecanoe and Tyler, too" was the Whig slogan, and their symbol was a barrel of hard cider. More than just a symbol, full cider barrels were present at all Whig rallies. Whether cider influenced the outcome

ROXBURY RUSSETS AT GREENWOOD FARM, NORTHFIELD, MASS.

PHOTO BY: CHARLIE OLCHOWSKI

of the election is unknown, but for the record, the "Tippecanoe and Tyler, too" ticket won by a landslide.

Cider at this point was at the peak of its popularity. Great orchards provided bountiful harvests, which in turn kept cider cheap and plentiful. Two social changes were at work, however, that would quickly reduce cider's popularity from the most common of beverages to almost complete obscurity.

DOWNFALL AND REVIVAL

The Industrial Revolution and Prohibition took a hard toll on the cider industry. Because of its availability, cider was inexpensive and often consumed in large quantities. Cideries also began adding rum to the already alcoholic cider, giving it quite a kick. Before too long, what had been a temperate and healthful drink became the cause of much concern. "It was a common saying that a cider drunkard was more cross and unbearable than any other" (*History of Wilton, New Hampshire, 1762 - 1888*).

Hard cider makes people awful mean when they're drunk and the choppers used to go out in the woods with a jug of hard cider in the late fall. They'd get to quarreling, and cut each other up with their axes.

(Walter Needham, *A Book of Country Things*)

Although it was actually the rum that caused these terrible fits of drunkenness, fermented cider became the lightning rod for the first temperance societies.

These temperance societies began developing around the time the Industrial Revolution started, and the combination was more than the cider industry could handle. America started to change from an agrarian society to an industrial one. Farmers left their orchards for job opportunities and the cosmopolitan life of the cities, and cider's foundation began to crumble. European immigrants – Italian, Polish, Dutch, Scandinavian, Irish, and German – were settling in the cities as well. Among the businesses these new immigrants brought with them were breweries and brewhouses, and they were ready to serve the clientele made up of the relocated farmers and cidermakers.

Cider was dealt the final blow in 1918, when the winter's freeze was so severe that entire orchards of cider trees were destroyed. Except for in a few rural apple growing areas mostly in New England, cidermaking stopped in America, while the commercial production of cider continued to thrive in Canada, Great Britain, and France.

For fifty years, American cidermaking teetered on the brink of extinction until the health-conscious trend of the 1960s renewed an interest in cider. People began shopping for more natural, less-processed foods as society became more aware of the role of nutrition as part of a healthier lifestyle. Americans embraced a "smaller is better" attitude, resulting in the emergence of small specialized companies that catered to specific needs and niche markets. These businesses were especially prevalent in the food and beverage industry.

After President Carter legalized homebrewing in 1978, many people discovered the joys of homebrewing and winemaking. It was only a matter of time before hard cider was rediscovered by a new generation of brewers.

By the beginning of the 1980s, several cider books made their way into print, although Vrest Orton's book *The American Cider Book* (Farrar, Straus and Giroux, 1973) had been trumpeting the virtues of cider for almost a decade. The growing interest in cider led to the import of commercial examples from Europe. American tourists returning from the United Kingdom and France began looking for imports like Bulmer's Sweet Woodpecker Cider and delicate French ciders from Normandy.

Enterprising Americans were not to be left behind. Brewpubs and microbreweries began offering hard cider on tap on a seasonal basis and even started bottling it for further distribution. However, the interest grew most at the grassroots level, in cellars and basements across the country. For homebrewers and winemakers who already had the necessary equipment at their disposal, making hard cider was as easy as buying a few gallons of freshly pressed sweet cider at the local supermarket, pouring it into whatever airtight container they had, adding yeast, and letting it ferment.

In 1991, a big step in the revival of cidermaking came with formal recognition of hard cider by the American Homebrewers Association. This organization for hobby brewers deemed cider worthy of its own category. By doing so, the AHA encourages members to educate themselves about cidermaking and enter the fruits of their labors in local and national competitions.

This grassroots effort is a proud reminder that the fruit does not fall far from the tree. Cider in the 1990s seems to be retaking its place in the history of our country right where it belongs, in the homes and dwellings of our citizens as a natural and healthy beverage made for personal consumption without interference from regulations and taxes. As well it should be. John Adams and those other radicals would be proud.

Starting Out

Autumn in New England is the most glorious of seasons. The brilliance of the turning leaves warms the crisp air as bright orange pumpkins, huge squash, and juicy apples of all varieties are gathered from fields and orchards. But a cidermaker need not call New England home in order to make a terrific hard cider. In fact, all you need is a minimum of equipment, some fresh pressed sweet cider, a cool and quiet place for the cider to ferment, and the satisfaction of knowing that you will be making the best hard cider around.

This section is written for YOU, the first-time cidermaker. Equipment to get started, sanitation, what you need to know about apple juice, what happens during fermentation, and finally bottling and enjoying your finished hard cider will all be discussed in plain, simple language. Making cider is simple, although the results are far from plain.

THE NECESSITIES

Don't be put off by thinking you need a massive hydraulic press or a limestone cellar to make fantastic hard cider. If you did, cider would not have become as popular as it was once. Remember that for centuries good hard cider was made by millions of people using archaic equipment with no more than a passing knowledge of what they were doing. The equipment available today through the many home-brewing and winemaking supply stores is far superior to what was used in cider's heyday. Besides, the colonists didn't have 1-800 numbers or climate-controlled dwellings to facilitate ordering and fermenting the stuff.

Equipment

Equipment that you will need to make cider is somewhat Spartan for a hobby. Everything you need for your first harvest is available at wine/beer-making supply stores (look in the yellow pages or in any wine/beermaking magazine). This is what you'll need for five gallons:

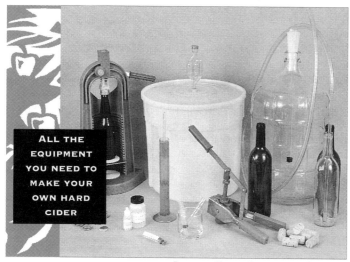

ALL THE EQUIPMENT YOU NEED TO MAKE YOUR OWN HARD CIDER

PHOTO BY: CHARLIE OLCHOWSKI AND DON PUGH

• a five-gallon glass carboy (large vessels used for bottled water)

• a five- to seven-gallon new food service-grade plastic bucket

• a siphoning set-up that includes a racking tube and tip, bottle filler, and about six feet of three eighths-inch (inside diameter) clear plastic tubing

• a four-foot section of five sixteenths-inch (inside diameter) clear plastic tubing

• a fermentation lock (also referred to as a water lock)

• a number 6 1/2 bored-rubber stopper

• a thermometer

• a wine or beer hydrometer with test jar

• acid testing kit or strips (optional)

• a bottle capper and clean caps

• a bottle brush and a carboy brush

• a set of measuring spoons, a measuring cup, and unscented household bleach (good cheap sanitizer)

• at least forty undamaged sixteen-ounce beer bottles or sixty sturdy twelve-ounce bottles, or others as long as they're returnable. These can be purchased new or, better still, collected from bars, parties, or recycling collection centers.

Very often most of the above gear is available as a package from homebrew supply stores and is less expensive than buying everything individually. Call stores for catalogs to see what they offer as well as shipping information. You can often find the glass car-

boys full of bottled water at supermarkets. Usually such locations make you pay for the water and place a deposit for the returnable bottle. Five gallon plastic containers are also often available but plastic can be easily scratched, giving unwanted bacteria a place to hide and making sanitation quite a challenge.

The Cellar

Hard cider is a living and breathing liquid that is affected for good or bad by light, vibration, and temperature. It is not some fragile little beverage that must be handled with kid gloves. Rather, cider will reflect the conditions in which it was fermented rather than be ruined by them.

The cellar can be situated wherever conditions are most favorable for the fermentation of good cider. Your cellar can be in the basement of a house, in an apartment closet, in a pantry, or even in an old reconditioned refrigerator. The size of your cellar isn't important, as long as there is enough room for the amount of cider you are fermenting. However, here are some guidelines for situating your cellar:

• Choose a spot that is relatively free from vibrations and out of the way of daily life. The less the cider is shaken, the clearer it will eventually become.

• Choose a spot that is relatively free from nasty smells. Storing painting supplies and cider in one general area is okay in a pinch; just make sure smelly cleaning rags and such aren't nearby unless you like a turpentine aroma to your cider.

• Keep the cider away from sunlight and/or bright lights. These will affect the taste of the finished cider. That's why beer and wine bottles are colored.

• Provide the cider with a cool environment in which to ferment. Cider does best in lager beer-type temperatures of 35 to 55 degrees F (2 to 13 degrees C), although fermenting at up to 68 degrees F (20 degrees C) is okay. The key word here is fluctuation. Sudden temperature swings affect one living thing as much as another, so keep the cider away from the boiler downstairs. However, gradual temperature changes that occur in many northern cellars, from the mid 60s in early autumn to the mid 30s in the dead of winter, are in fact beneficial to the young cider.

Taken in sum, you can see that there are many places in a house or apartment that could qualify as a satisfactory cellar. You, the budding cidermaker, must decide what is realistic and practical. Remember, cider is hardy and resilient, and it takes more than a few bumps to make it turn out less than perfect.

THE IMPORTANCE OF SANITATION

Prior to the advent of the microscope and the findings of Louis Pasteur, the process of fermentation was conducted at best by following tried and true methods passed down through the years. Nobody really understood what was happening underneath the foaming cap of a barrel of turning cider. We now know that fermentation is akin to an all-you-can-eat buffet with everyone invited; the foods are the sugars and other nutrients in the sweet juice, and the guests are the swarms of different yeast strains, bacteria, and other ravenous micro-organisms that eat until they drop.

Your goal is to make great cider. Your role as cidermaker requires that you keep out the unwanted guests that will foul your cider with bizarre smells and sour tastes. It's your cider and your party. By practicing good sanitation, you can enforce the rule of "invited guests only" and assuredly make great cider every harvest season.

Good sanitation is neither complicated nor expensive. An obsession with sterility is not a part of the cider experience. Once clean, sanitizing the equipment is as easy as a soak in a bucket of water and sanitizing solution and as inexpensive as a penny per five gallons.

Cleaners and Sanitizers

• Bleach (plain and unscented): Super strong only compared to the concentration that you will be preparing, household bleach is chlorine diluted to five percent of full strength before it is sold.

A solution of one-forth cup of bleach to five gallons of warm or cold water is effective as a cleaner for used or stained glass carboys. A loosening scrub with a long-handled nylon brush and an hour-long soak will do the trick. Rinse well with hot water to remove traces of bleach before filling with cider. Since carboys are not tempered against thermal shock, it is important to start your rinse with warm water and slowly increase the temperature until the water is hot.

A solution of two tablespoons of bleach to five gallons of warm or cold water is effective as a sanitizer for cleaned glass carboys and other clean glass and plastic equipment only if they are totally immersed for at least one half hour. Equipment is easily sanitized by making the solution in your five- to seven-gallon plastic bucket then tossing in the plastic hoses, funnel, hydrometer, etc., that you'll be using. Kick back for a thirty-minute snooze as your equipment air dries before use. Don't be paranoid about a bacteriological coup d'état in your fermenter. This is as complicated as it gets.

• B-Brite: This excellent product is available in all homebrew supply shops and is widely used by homebrewers, and home wine and cidermakers. It is more expensive than bleach but has the advantage of killing micro-organisms on contact, thus no waiting (or snoozing) before your equipment is sanitized. A solution of two tablespoons of B-Brite to five gallons of water is an effective cleaner and sanitizer. A rinse in running tap water is required following a dip in B-Brite. Note that B-Brite is a sanitizer for equipment only and is not to be used to eliminate micro-organisms in the cider.

• Campden tablets, sodium or potassium metabisulfite: Basically these are all the same thing. They work by releasing sulfur dioxide into an acidic environment such as apple or grape juice to prevent fermentation and somewhat "sanitize" the juice without being sanitizers. They are used primarily by wine-makers and very sparingly by cidermakers. They are used primarily to keep wooden casks and barrels sweet when not filled with cider. (See "Large-container Fermentation" in chapter nine for more information.)

There are other sanitizing and cleaning products on the market, so be very careful with what you use (household soaps will leave foul-tasting residues and films) and especially what you might accidentally mix (these products are usually highly toxic). Nontoxic household soaps may be used around the cellar to clean up spills or grime on countertops and tables. It is also a good idea to have a small spray bottle (clearly write "bleach" on it) that you can fill with fresh bleach sanitizing solution to quickly spritz and wipe up spills as they occur.

You can see that keeping your equipment sanitized and your cellar clean is an easy but extremely important part of successful cidermaking. You must be consistent in keeping the uninvited guests out of your all-you-can-eat buffet. If ever the saying "an ounce of prevention is worth a pound of cure" had special meaning for a particular group of people, it would be to those who diligently enforce the "invited guests only" rule.

EIGHT STEPS TO GREAT CIDER

The following steps will outline the simplicity in making your first batch of fermented cider. To make consistently super cider, the sweet cider must be healthy, the fermentation must take place in clean and sanitary surroundings, and the fermenting cider must be well sealed with a water lock, as contact with air might turn your cider to vinegar.

1. Fill a five-gallon glass carboy with four and a half gallons of sweet cider.

2. Add one-half to one cup of sugar for each gallon of sweet cider.

3. Add a bottle of active yeast to the sweet cider in the carboy to start the fermentation process. Active yeast come in liquid or dried form, are a snap to prepare, and work like a sourdough starter for bread. After adding the yeast, lightly cover the top of the carboy with plastic wrap.

4. Within a week the cider will be working. Remove the wrap to let the foam, scum, and bits of apple cascade out of the container as the cider cleanses itself. Wipe down the sides of the container daily.

5. This vigorous fermentation subsides within a few weeks. Wipe down the container thoroughly and top off the cider to within two inches of the top with fresh sweet cider. Seal the carboy with the number 6 1/2 bored-rubber stopper and a water lock to prevent outside air from getting in.

6. Forget about the cider for a while (about four weeks) as the cider slowly ferments and begins to clear.

7. Between twelve and sixteen weeks after adding the yeast to your sweet cider, the fermenting cider can be transferred into a clean container or left as is to age and mellow.

8. Eight weeks after transferring to a clean container (approximately twenty weeks after adding the yeast), your smooth and clear cider is ready to be bottled and, more importantly, tasted.

That's all there is to it! There are, of course, more details to learn with each batch you make, but the hardest thing about making cider is waiting to kick back and enjoy a few bottles of nature's finest with family and friends.

The Harvest & The Juice

Making hard cider is a seasonal avocation that reflects the influences of the natural world as much as those of the individual cidermaker. In this you feel an inner satisfaction that comes from working with the fruits of nature to craft a beverage that is not only exquisite but also uniquely tailored to your own personal tastes. Regardless of what style or type you decide to make, all ciders go through many of the same steps as they proceed from ripened apples to finished hard cider.

Apple trees are slow and steady growers: they blossom and fruit the same way. The firmer and more-flavorful, late-season apples often don't really reach their peak ripeness until at least first frost or even first hard frost. This long season almost guarantees a well-ripened harvest, much to the delight of cidermakers who are happy to proclaim that every year is a good year for cider.

Apple trees are massively shaped with gnarled downward-spreading limbs that facilitate picking. Orchards send out pickers to twist the fruit off the tree or to gather the just-fallen fruit during a period called "the drop".

The apples are then sorted by appearance and size (not by taste) into first-grade quality for retail sale, second-grade quality for pies or applesauce, and cider-grade quality for pressing and juice. A respectable mill operator will include only healthy, albeit less than picture-perfect apples, in his cider. Neither damaged nor rotting fruits are desired, for these are sure to contain high amounts of unhealthy bacteria and toxins.

First- and second-grade apples are then refrigerated to retard further maturing before they are boxed or bagged and sent off to markets around the world. Cider-grade apples, however, are left to mellow in a protected and well-ventilated area for up to two weeks where they become sweeter, easier to grind, and juicier as they ripen.

COMMERCIAL CRUSHING AND PRESSING

Before being ground to a pulp and pressed, the apples are thoroughly washed to remove traces of muck, spray residues (the waxy coating on apples is wild yeast called the bloom), and other things that don't belong in cider.

A mechanical drum grinder crushes the apples to applesauce consistency then pumps the cleaned and mashed fruit into a press bag of burlap or nylon. These applesauce "pillows" are framed by squared forms that look like dresser drawers without bottoms. When full, the form is removed, a flat rack is placed on top of the bag, and the next bag is framed and filled. On and on this stack of apple-filled pillows called the cheese is constructed until it reaches the desired height, usually ten to fifteen layers. Hydraulic power is then applied slowly and steadily in a series of stops and starts for clearer juice and greater yield. Although screw presses (used to press much softer fruit such as grapes) have a romantic look about them, they cannot match the tremendous pressures exerted by commercial hydraulic presses (up to 2,200 pounds per square inch) or the efficiency hydraulic presses can achieve (around three gallons of juice per bushel).

After every last drop of a harvest's essence is extracted, the sweet cider is pumped into a refrigerated stainless-steel settling tank for an overnight stay. By the next morning, the larger and heavier pieces of pulp will have settled to the bottom. At this stage the sweet cider will be bottled in retail-sized containers and sold as fresh pressed apple cider. This is when our fun begins!

THE JUICE

A distinct advantage that cidermakers have over winemakers and brewers is the ease with which we ready our raw materials for fermentation. Winemakers must destem, crush, and press their grapes to get juice. Brewers have to crush, boil, strain, and cool grains, hops, and water before adding yeast. The aspiring cidermaker may pick up fresh sweet apple cider at the local supermarket in handy one-gallon plastic jugs or fill up carboys at the thousands of cidermills at farm stands throughout the vast apple growing areas of the United States and Canada. In either case, the hard work of getting the juice out of the apples is done. No purple juice stains on your clothes and toes, no sticky kitchen brewery mess. The cidermaker's role is to ensure the quality of the sweet cider used for his or her own hard cider. Sick juice makes sick cider. So as head of quality control, you will want to find and purchase only fresh and unadulterated sweet cider, then test and possibly adjust the levels of sugar, acid, and tannin to ensure a healthy and well-balanced whole. All this is done with a few basic instruments, keen eyes, and a determined nose.

How sweet it is! The rise in popularity of fresh juices and juice blends means that it is almost impossible not to find freshly pressed sweet apple cider in the produce sec-

RONALD HEADLEY PICKS UP APPLES OFF THE GROUND DURING THE PERIOD CALLED "THE DROP" AT PINE HILL ORCHARDS.

PHOTO BY: CHARLIE OLCHOWSKI

tion of most major supermarkets during the apple harvest season. Talk to the produce managers of area supermarkets and find out if and when they stock fresh sweet cider. Ask whether it contains any preservatives, which extends the shelf life of the sweet cider by preventing fermentation. Preservative-free sweet cider is usually fresher since the shelf life is shortened, plus the lack of preservatives ensures a quicker start to your fermentation

When sweet cider starts arriving in the stores, shop around and make notes about freshness (expiration dates on the cartons) and price. Buy some to take home and drink, then test for sugar and acid (see p. 15). The sweet cider sold in supermarkets is composed of the most abundant apple varieties available, which usually means a sweet and aromatic blend of our most common eating apples (Delicious, Gravenstein, McIntosh, Jonathan, etc.). This "orchard blend" has moderate sugar and acid levels with little tannin and may need minor additions. If free of preservatives and freshly pressed, supermarket-purchased sweet cider is certainly more than adequate for making hard cider, and it's so convenient.

The same standards of quality apply to the purchase of sweet cider in a health-food store, although the cider available here tends to be preservative free. There is also more to choose from as some stores stock fresh varietal sweet ciders (pressed from a single apple variety) when they become available during the season. Prices are a bit higher than in supermarkets, but health-food stores have been, and continue to be, beacons of hope to those who are unable to procure their juice from any other source. If anything, the more expensive yet more flavorful varietal sweet ciders are best used to perk up the low-acid yet reasonably priced supermarket ciders.

Most of us live within a short drive of "apple country" — the farm stands located among the apple orchards and the cidermills — and can go right to the source for our raw materials. Good apples grow almost everywhere in the continental United States (except the extreme south and parts of California) and in southern Canada. Finding a clean, well-run orchard and cidermill is no more a chore than a pleasant stop during a lazy late summer or early fall drive through the country.

The newspaper is a great place to locate nearby orchards and mills. The Sunday travel or entertainment sections often do seasonal features on "country living" and provide information about area farm stands. The cooking or food sections will often name specific orchards and apple varieties with the arrival of harvest cuisine. Call the local Chamber of Commerce or Bureau of Tourism for free maps and scenic "apple trails."

Regardless of how you get there, you are able to extend your influence as head of quality control by purchasing direct from the producer. See what the different farm stands offer. Check out the premises and the presshouse, if possible, to evaluate general cleanliness. Use your eyes and nose, get a feel for the place. Talk to the people running the business, mention your interest in making a bit of the hard stuff. More than likely, they'll give you the straight scoop about what apples are the best to use this season and when they'll be pressing the most flavorful apples.

MANUEL SALOMAN POURS APPLES INTO THE GRINDER AT BOULDER FRUIT EXPRESS IN BOULDER, COLO.

PHOTO BY: ELIZABETH GOLD

Another advantage of buying direct is the obvious freshness and lack of preservatives in the juice. A better price is also possible, especially if you bring your own clean carboys to be filled on the spot (or make arrangements for this to be done at a later date). You needn't worry too much about the specific apples going into the juice. The goal of the search is to find a well-run, clean, and friendly cidermill that sells fresh sweet cider using a variety of sound apples.

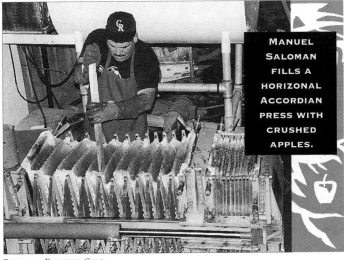

MANUEL SALOMAN FILLS A HORIZONAL ACCORDIAN PRESS WITH CRUSHED APPLES.

PHOTO BY: ELIZABETH GOLD

Okay, you're back from the supermarket/health-food store/cidermill. You've got ten gallons of the best sweet cider you could find in handy one-gallon plastic jugs, and you want to make two five-gallon batches of cider: one a lighter style with a natural alcohol level of about 6 percent by volume (4.7 percent alcohol by weight) and the other a more robust style of about 9 percent by volume (7.1 percent alcohol by weight). Before letting hungry hoards of yeast run wild through the sweet cider, you need to measure the levels of acids and sugars and possibly adjust them to have as balanced a juice as possible prior to fermentation. Delicious hard cider can be made without measuring or adjusting anything in your sweet cider. But better and more consistently successful hard cider can be had by making sure that the primary elements of taste in your sweet cider are all in balance with one another. Balanced taste is the mark of a well-made cider and it is a goal that is easily achieved.

SUGARS, ACID, AND TANNIN

Natural sugars make sweet cider sweet, and when digested by yeast, make hard cider hard. So by measuring the amount of sugar in the juice, the cidermaker will also know the potential alcohol content of the finished cider. This is very important, not for ridiculous high-test bragging rights but because finished cider must have a certain alcohol content to keep for any length of time.

A hydrometer is used to test the sugar content. This instrument is about as big around as a test tube with a more slender calibrated top stem and measures the specific gravity, which is the amount of solids (most of them sugars) in the juice. The more sugar in the juice, the higher the hydrometer will float and the higher the reading. To take a reading, open the jug of sweet cider. Pour yourself a glass, take a swig, then fill the test jar almost to the top with 60-degree-F (16-degree-C) juice. The temperature of the juice is important in order to get an accurate reading. Float the hydrometer in the juice and read the specific gravity. Keep a record of this to compare to later readings. All this information, as well as any other factors pertaining to the life of your cider and the activity in your cellar, should be documented in a cider log. Try as you might, it is all but impossible to remember all the factors contributing to a great (or maybe not so great) cider. A well-detailed log is invaluable to repeat the steps for a superior cider as well as to avoid past errors.

Many factors contribute to the amount of sugar in the juice from year to year. Weather is the single most important factor. A hot and dry season will fully ripen the apples and raise their sugar content. A cool and wet season, on the other hand, will produce fruits with higher-acid and lower-sugar levels. Other factors include the overall health of the orchard, the harvest date, and the apple varieties used. Under normal conditions, the juice of North American apples will have a specific gravity between 1.040 and 1.050. Fully fermented, undosed cider (no sugars added to the juice) will have a finished alcohol level of around 6 percent by volume (4.7 percent by weight). This level may not entirely safeguard your cider against unwanted yeast activity even after bottling. Some organisms survive quite well in lower-alcohol ciders, especially if the storage temperatures rise above 60 degrees F (16 degrees C) during the course of the season. Naturally made cider is a living thing and must be stabilized to prevent possible spoilage. A delicate, low-alcohol cider may be made, stored, and consumed without hesitation only if kept well chilled or if a preservative, such as Campden tablets, is added prior to bottling (one crushed tablet per gallon). Otherwise, bring the specific gravity up to at least 1.060 because higher levels of alcohol make the liquid environment much less hospitable to unwanted yeast.

Adjusting the specific gravity is easy, just remember to keep track of how much sugar you add. To raise the specific gravity of one gallon of juice 5 degrees, 2.25 ounces of granulated sugar must be added. This means that to adjust the specific gravity 20 degrees from 1.047 to 1.067 for each gallon in a five-gallon carboy, the amount needed is 4 x 2.25 ounces sugar = 9 ounces sugar per gallon, or as an experienced cidermaker would say, "a rounded cup per gallon." The sugar may be stirred directly into the juice in the carboy (remember to leave one-half gallon of juice out of every carboy for later additions) or it may be dissolved into a syrup with a small amount of hot water or cider for easier mixing.

Malic acid in apples is what gives zing to the sweet cider. It balances the sugars in the juice and makes it refreshing to drink rather than syrupy sweet and dull. After fermentation, acid levels diminish as the cider mellows but the acid continues to balance the alcohol and helps naturally protect the finished cider. Since North American table apples normally contain an ideal level of acidity, the cidermaker can skip the task of treating and adjusting for acid unless a large percentage of the juice was pressed from the low-acid Red Delicious. In that case, an acid-testing kit available at homebrew supply stores is recommended. Follow the simple instructions included with such kits and adjust the juice accordingly.

The easiest way to understand the taste of tannin is to suck on a used tea bag or bite into a piece of stem from a bunch of grapes. Tannin provides long-term structure to finished hard cider as well as a pleasant dry finish. Sweet cider made from true cider and crab apples has enough tannin to stand on its own. Sweet cider from table apples, on the other hand, needs to be adjusted with one teaspoon of tannin powder for every five gallons of sweet cider. Tannin powder is available at all homebrew supply stores.

Two five-gallon carboys of juice have been measured and adjusted and are ready for fermentation, one as a delicate cider and one as a robust cider. All that is needed is the addition of the invited guests: a known and uncontaminated yeast strain bred specifically to convert sugars to alcohol in the process called fermentation. The guests are ready to arrive at the all-you-can-eat buffet.

Fermentation

Don't be intimidated by thoughts of having to don clean suits and work with petri dishes. There are many suitable varieties of pure yeast cultures available in shops in either dried or liquid form. The cidermaker must do nothing more than prepare a yeast starter for the store-bought yeast, dump it into the carboy full of juice when ready, and give it a good swirl (explained on p. 18). An understanding of yeast, our invited guest, and an appreciation of the living process of fermentation will make you an attuned and superior cidermaker.

Fermentation is the process in which yeast convert sugars in a medium into carbon dioxide (CO_2) and ethyl alcohol before going dormant and settling. Although yeast from the species Saccharomyces are grouped as fungi, this process can be somewhat imagined as a group of one-cell organisms feasting on sugar (whether glucose in grape juice, fructose in apple juice, or maltose in beer) as they split

and multiply throughout the juice. As the sugar is consumed, alcohol and CO_2 are produced until the yeast run out of food. The yeast then go dormant and drop to the bottom of the carboy. The fermentation of cider proceeds in stages that may not be too sharply defined. Remember that factors such as the type of yeast used and the temperature of the cider's surroundings contribute to the length of time it takes to ferment cider.

Primary fermentation tweaks the senses as the sweet/sharp aroma of fermenting cider engulfs the cellar. A week or so after the yeast have been pitched (added) into the sweet cider, bubbles start rising until an almost rolling simmer engages the contents of the carboy as CO_2 is released and alcohol is produced. After about one month, fermentation slows to a steady blub-blub-blub of CO_2 through the water lock. Usually sometime between Thanksgiving and Christmas, all the sugar has been converted to alcohol. The yeast go dormant because their food supply has been depleted, and the cider starts to clear when the yeast settle to the bottom of the carboy.

CIDER FERMENTING IN A GLASS CARBOY

PHOTO BY: CHARLIE OLCHOWSKI AND DON PUGH

The young cider is now alcoholic and dry with a somewhat sharp aftertaste.

Secondary fermentation occurs after or sometimes during primary fermentation as lactic acid bacteria, already present in the juice, ferment the sharp-tasting malic acid at temperatures below 55 degrees F (13 degrees C). At higher temperatures, around 70 degrees F (21 degrees C), these same bacteria can cause awful smells and tastes (see chapter seven, "Troubleshooting"). Your acid-level tester will show a steady decrease in acidity as the young cider develops a smooth taste and becomes oh-so pleasant to drink.

Two factors that cause the fermentation process to slow are the depletion of the food source by the yeast, since they've consumed most of the sugars, and the subsequent action of the increased alcohol levels on the yeast. In the same way that pickles are preserved in a brine too salty to support any kind of harmful micro-organism, increased levels of alcohol diminish and finally stop fermentation because the cells go dormant and fall slowly to the bottom. This procedure is used in the manufacture of port, since fermentation is stopped by adding brandy to the wine while still sweet with unfermented sugars. Fermentation is the life cycle of the invited guests. They arrive at the big buffet, chow down as much sugar as is available while burping out alcohol and CO_2. When the table is clean they settle down for a nap, not much

different than having the relatives over for Sunday dinner.

A clean and healthy fermentation is the goal of the cidermaker. This is assured through conditions conducive to a good fermentation, so that the yeast you use will flourish and provide the nuances of taste that you desire. Be assured, though, cider is so adaptable and easy to make that you could use almost any of the cultured wine or beer yeast strains or even wild yeast with unknown characteristics to turn your juice into really good cider. But for beginning cidermakers it is best to know a bit more about the yeast you use.

YEAST

There are thousands of known yeast strains, but precious few of the genus Saccharomyces are able to convert simple sugars to alcohol and carbon dioxide. Of those used for cider, wine, and beer, it is important to remember that these living organisms all have unique flavors to contribute to the finished cider and somewhat different requirements for optimum fermentation. Therefore, two factors need to be considered in choosing the best yeast for a particular batch of cider: the temperature at which fermentation will take place and the style of cider being made.

Currently, "cider" yeast is not available in homebrew or wine supply stores. You have the option of using ale or lager beer yeasts or any kind of white wine yeast which are available in these stores. Dried yeasts are available in small sealed packets, containing enough granules for a five-gallon batch. From these packets a yeast starter may be made that will work quicker and be more effective in overcoming any other competing yeast strains.

Preparing a yeast starter is easy, but proper sanitation must be followed or you risk contamination. You will need a sixteen-ounce or twenty-two-ounce glass bottle, a kettle filled with water, a six-ounce can or bottle of pasteurized apple juice at room temperature, a packet of yeast, a rubber band, and a hermetically sealed condom (don't laugh, they're great for keeping bacteria out while allowing the CO_2 room to expand). First you must rehydrate the yeast to slowly wake it from its dormant state. If it is just tossed in the "cold shock," the number of viable yeast cells will be substantially reduced and their ability to quickly and efficiently ferment your cider will be weakened. In other words, you've got to literally warm up your invited guests. To do this, simply sprinkle your pack of yeast into a half glassful of 105- to 114-degree-F (41- to 46-degree-C) water.

In the meantime, put the bottle in the kettle, cover with water, and boil for fifteen minutes to sterilize. Drain it and let it cool for a few minutes. Open the juice and carefully pour it into the bottle ... no drips or dribbles. Follow this with the half glass of rehydrated yeast using the same steadiness of hand. Give the bottle a quick swirl, attach the condom to the open neck of the bottle, and secure with a rubber band.

You have now created your own mini-cider fermenter. In a day or two, the yeast will have started to convert the sugars to alcohol and CO_2, which will cause the condom to expand and a layer of bubbles to be visible on the surface of the juice. At or near this point, the amount of viable yeast cells will be at its maximum, so carefully swirl the contents of the bottle to loosen any clinging cells, remove the condom, and pour carefully into the waiting five-gallon carboy of sweet cider. Give the carboy a swirl to mix in and aerate the already-working cells, and soon your sweet cider will be fermenting.

If your cellar happens to be a hallway closet or somewhere that is room temperature, an ale yeast should be used. This beer yeast works well when fermenting cider at temperatures above 60 degrees F (16 degrees C). The yeast will work quickly because of the temperature, will retain much of the apple/fruity aromas and tastes, and will finish dry with a slight ale taste. A nice quaffer to dispense from a keg at summer parties.

If your cellar is cooler than 60 degrees F (16 degrees C), ideally between 45 and 55 degrees F (7 to 13 degrees C) you may use lager beer yeast, white wine, or champagne yeast. Fermenting at cool temperatures takes a bit longer, but the finished cider is usually smoother and certainly clearer. Lager yeast will work somewhat like the ale yeast in retaining the apple taste, but the finish will be more refined — a good choice if you like your cider with a hint of sweetness. Many white wine yeasts can be used. Each one is said to leave different nuances in the finished wine (or cider). They differ from beer yeasts in that they convert more sugar to alcohol and are used for stronger cider. The effects on taste are more noticeable as well. The taste is more winelike, the cider is drier, and the acidity more noticeable — less of a quaffer and more of a sipper. Champagne yeast makes superb cider. It takes a little longer to get going, but it makes great stuff, is crystal clear, and is bone dry with tiny swirling bubbles.

Regardless of the yeast you use, make sure to use the proper amount to ferment the quantity of juice you have. It is far better to use a little more to ensure that your invited guests will quickly dominate whatever other yeasts happen to drop in. The folks at your local homebrew or winemaking supply shop should be able to tell you how much of a particular yeast you will need to ferment your sweet cider.

SULFUR DIOXIDE

Sulfur dioxide (SO_2) is used primarily in winemaking to eliminate the wild yeasts and bacteria in a vat of fresh juice prior to pitching the desired yeast. The use of SO_2 in the fermentation of cider is controversial and is the subject of lively discussion. If anything, SO_2 isn't as effective before fermentation as it is after. Preventative measures such as purchasing healthy sweet cider and using plenty of good, fresh yeast to ensure quick domination over uninvited guests are key to a good start for the cider. However, if you are tolerant of sulfites you will find that the addition of SO_2 to the finished cider before bottling is beneficial in protecting a low-alcohol cider from wild yeasts. Some wild yeasts are alcohol tolerant and may contribute off flavors or aromas to the bottled cider if combined with other factors such as warm storage temperatures. Sulfites are also used to stop yeast activity. Stopping a fermentation before all the sugar is consumed creates a sweet or off-dry cider. Which means the cider will have just a touch of residual sweetness to keep it from being mouth-puckeringly dry.

Valid arguments can be made for both sides. Nobody wants to put more preservatives in our foods, but then again, why risk losing an entire batch of cider if the preservative may be safely added? Plenty of information is available about sulfites in foods and wines. The books about wine listed in the bibliography are particularly good sources of information. I suggest getting the facts and making your own decision because it is your cider.

If you decide to add sulfite to your juice, the task of measuring out SO_2 is simplified by purchasing potassium metabisulfite, which is sold as Campden tablets at supply stores. Crush two tablets per gallon of sweet cider to release the SO_2 (it will smell like rotten eggs) and stir in. This will give a concentration of 100 parts per million, which will effectively prevent the growth of most yeast strains and bacteria. Sodium metabisulfite cannot distinguish between wanted and unwanted yeast, so if you decide to sterilize the sweet juice before adding the healthy yeast starter, remember to wait twenty-four hours for the chemical effects to diminish. Otherwise, your pure yeast strain will be destroyed as well. If you are using SO_2 to stabilize a fermented low-alcohol cider or one that has been fermented to dry and then sweetened up, bottle immediately after the addition of the crushed tablets. The disagreeable odors will dissipate over time.

CLARIFYING AND FINING

The activity in your carboy is winding down a month or two after pitching the yeast when the winter months approach. Small bubbles rise slowly through the murky new (freshly fermented, but still rough tasting) cider. Through the glass, you can see sediment start to cake on the bottom as the yeast, having eaten almost all the available sugar, settle and go dormant. Although the cider is now alcoholic, it is a long way from a fine, smooth beverage.

This is the adolescent period for your new cider. Like a teenager, the cider is angular, unbalanced, and its complexion leaves a lot to be desired. But don't worry because by late winter (four or five months after pitching the yeast) the cider will be brilliantly clear. All you need to do is be patient. The bubbling in the airlock will slow and then cease altogether. The only activity may be a few tiny bubbles rising ever so slowly from the bottom of the carboy. Replace the light sanitizing solution in the airlock every few weeks and never let it go dry. At this stage the cider is very susceptible to acetification (bacteria that live in the air can turn your cider into cider vinegar).

Your cider will lose its murky appearance, become translucent, and then finally clear over a period of a few weeks or a month. After the yeast have settled, the process of clearing is greatly aided by very cool or even cold temperatures, preferably between 30 and 45 degrees F (-1 and 7 degrees C). This is easily accomplished by moving the cider to an unheated area of the house (don't let it freeze) during the winter or by placing the entire carboy in a utility refrigerator (or cold-store) the same way a homebrewer would lager a German-style beer. Even without these low temperatures, the cider will clear to a very reasonable degree, leaving at worst only a slight haze in your cider. If you are insistent on a brilliantly clear liquid, many fining agents are available in supply shops. These work by either dissolving the minute solids in the cider or, conversely, by attaching themselves to the solids making their greater weight fall to the bottom of the carboy. Fining agents include pectic enzyme, gelatin, and others sold under their respective brand names. Read and follow the instructions carefully, but keep in mind that these products will also remove flavor elements in the cider — a ridiculous price to pay for perfect clarity, in my opinion

Notice that filtering the cider is not mentioned, and with good reason. One reason is that the price of a commercial filter is prohibitive, another is that homemade filters over oxidize cider, making it turn dark and taste caramelized. As stated time and again, hard cider is ridiculously easy to make. It will most certainly clear by itself if healthy and given time. So relax while your cider and Mother Nature do their thing!

BULK AGING

For about one month after your cider clears, it should be left to quietly bulk age in the carboy. Like beer, wine, or even mom's hearty soups or stews, a little time goes a long way to ensure that the flavors mellow and blend into a harmonious whole. This does bring up the question of whether the cidermaker should siphon the cider off the sediment in a process called racking or racking off the lees (sediment), and if so, how often?

Many accomplished cidermakers rack their cider two or three times prior to bottling, leaving less and less sediment behind as the solids fall and the cider clears. This is done by inserting a three-eighths-inch-diameter clear rubber hose (part of your basic equipment) attached to a rigid plastic stick into the bottom of a raised carboy of cider. Note that the opening of the hose is staggered at least one inch up the stick so that it sucks up cider, not sediment. An empty, sanitized carboy is placed below the full carboy or fermenter. The top of the empty carboy should be lower than the bottom of your full fermenter. Then siphon the cider out of the

full carboy and into the empty one. Two different techniques can be used to siphon your cider. The least complicated method is mouth suction. Place the end of the plastic tube attached to the plastic stick into your cider then suck on the other end as if it were a giant straw. When you taste cider, clamp shut the end that was in your mouth and lower it into the empty carboy. Release the clamp and watch the cider flow. Push the tube to the bottom of the filling carboy to limit unwanted stirring and aeration.

The alternate method is a bit more complex. Fill the three-eighths-inch rubber hose with water and cover the end that will go into the empty carboy with your sanitized thumb (or clamp it shut). After placing the end attached to the rubber stick into your cider, lower the other end below the bottom of the full carboy and remove your thumb. (Have a spare bowl or pot ready to catch the water.) The water will flow out, siphoning the cider behind it. Stop the flow before wasting any of your cider by placing your thumb over the opening or clamping the tube shut. Put the tube into the empty carboy and let the cider run. Again, put the tube in the bottom of the filling carboy to limit unwanted aeration. Fill the ullage (airspace between the top of the newly siphoned cider and the top of the carboy) with cider from another container or with sanitized water, and fit the full carboy with an fermentation lock.

Although seemingly harmless, racking cider numerous times does carry risks, especially if the cidermaker has opted for a natural cider without the addition of sulfites or Campden tablets to somewhat protect the cider from bacteria. Even brief contact with the air will slightly oxidize the light-colored cider, browning it slightly (evident when you leave a cut apple exposed to air). You also run the risk again of acetification.

Cider does quite well if left undisturbed in the same container during the fermentation and bulk-aging process. It does equally well if racked just once after fermentation slows and only tiny bubbles make their way up through the still murky cider. Besides the final racking into a sanitized bucket just before bottling, this is all the racking a natural cider needs. Just leave the cider alone as much as possible to bulk age until it is time to bottle. The cider will be fine, resting and evolving as it gains complexity like many champagnes and sparkling wines.

Bottling & Aging

ottling time is as joyous a spring occasion as the return of baseball or the planting of early peas. At six months, the "teenage" cider is quite drinkable although somewhat sharp and unbalanced. Don't panic, cider needs to be siphoned into sanitized bottles and closed off to air, then allowed to rest for a few months to let the flavors mellow and the edges soften. If you've got a respectable amount of cider that needs bottling, remember that family and friends are usually more than happy to help wash, sanitize, fill, and cap the bottles, in exchange for some finished cider of course. Organize a potluck dinner to go with the flowing fresh young cider and you'll be a two-time hero — for throwing a great party and for helping in the revival of this great beverage.

BOTTLES, CORKS, AND CAPS

Cidermakers have always recycled their bottles from vintage to vintage. Now that others are catching up, it is much easier and cheaper to acquire them. Instead of picking through bar-room trash for empties or paying for brand new bottles, the recycling center has become the preferred way to build a good collection of fairly clean and cheap bottles. In states with a bottle bill, the liquor stores handle the beer empties that usually must be returned clean. The stores can only charge you the amount of the refund, five cents per bottle. A big liquor store handles all kinds of beer brands, thus all kinds of bottle sizes, shapes, and colors.

The sturdiest bottles available are long-neck bar bottles with a smooth lip for a crimped cap, although any

refundable bottle is fine. Most hold twelve ounces, although cider looks great in the respectable and sometimes available sixteen-ounce size. Another good bottle is the fairly new twenty-two-ounce size. In any case, you can get what you need at little cost and hassle. If you live in a town with a dump or a transfer station, you can find wine bottles (for noncarbonated cider) and beer empties as well as the more treasured champagne bottles (nonrefundable and the most expensive to buy new). Just hang out on a Saturday morning in front of the "colored glass" recycling bins and relieve people of their empties.

However you acquire your bottles, visually check them for nicks and chips. Wash them in the dishwasher or hot soapy water, taking care to use a bottle brush for any stubborn spots, and rinse in plain water. The clean bottles must then be sanitized with a bleach solution or B-Brite, and the tops covered with plastic film until ready to fill.

Caps and corks are the final precaution against air-breathing, uninvited guests. Always use new closures and sanitized caps to seal the fruits of your labor. Boil caps in water for five minutes and leave them in the covered pot until you're ready to crimp them on the bottles. A ten-minute boil is recommended for corks in order to soften them up properly.

Caps may be used to seal off either finished still (noncarbonated) hard cider or cider that is primed and soon to become sparkling (carbonated). All beer bottles and most champagne bottles can be capped using a one-size bottle cap. French champagne bottles, which are thicker around the top, are the exception. They can be sealed (as can all other champagne bottles) with plastic champagne stoppers and then wired down.

Corks are used to finish off wine bottles filled with still cider only (the pressure building up inside a sparkler would pop the cork right out). Unlike the one-size-fits-all caps, corks come in all different diameters and lengths, although the number 9-size cork will fit almost all standard wine bottles. Remember that corks are far from airtight and their very nature allows slight interaction between air and liquid, resulting in a maturing or mellowing of tastes. For this reason, be wary of corking lighter-style ciders because their delicate taste and balance may be adversely affected. More robust styles take much better to corking and are able to age for a year or two, deepening in color and taste.

Cappers and/or corkers are used to crimp the caps onto the bottles or force the corks into the necks. There is quite a selection to choose from, but only a few are worth getting. If you are on a tight budget and are only capping small batches, a two-handled crimper will do. However, after a few batches the rivets will loosen, or you'll tire of not having a free hand to lift a cider to your lips. The best device is a bench capper or corker. These attach to a counter or are heavy and freestanding. The bottle is placed underneath, a cap is placed on top or a cork is placed in the funnel, and with one twirl of the lever the bottle is corked or capped. Mine is from Italy and made of hard, bright red plastic. It has attachments for either caps or corks and adjusts to different bottle heights. It cost thirty-five dollars ten years ago but has been used to finish off close to 2,000 gallons of fermented beverages and looks as good as new. A good capper may be your most expensive piece of equipment but the best investment in the long and short run.

BOTTLING STILL OR SPARKLING CIDER

Finally, it's time! The cider has a dry taste and has completely fermented out (a constant hydrometer reading between 0.950 and 1.005 should confirm this). Sanitized and ready are the bottles, siphoning sticks, tubes, caps/corks and five- to ten-gallon siphoning bucket, along with the capper, and of course, a friend or two to help or learn.

For sparkling cider, a small amount of sugar must be added to the dry cider before it is capped (this process is called priming). Be very accurate in measuring the amounts of sugar given in the two methods outlined because even a little too much will result in either gushers or worse, cider grenades (no joking matter).

To prime (carbonate) bottle by bottle, one level half teaspoon of sugar is funneled into each twelve-ounce bottle before flat cider is siphoned in and the bottle is capped. This is a good method for priming smaller amounts of cider (gallon-jug batches) or for minimizing the exposure to air, since the cider may be racked directly from the fermenter (or gallon jug) to the bottle.

Many cidermakers and homebrewers find it easier to prime an entire batch of cider at one time, especially larger quantities. To do this, a measured sugar syrup is mixed into a clear cider that has just been racked off its lees. For five gallons of cider, boil a half cup of cane or corn sugar together with and a pint of water for five minutes. Let this mixture cool (in the pot with the lid still on) before mixing with your cider. Pour the cooled syrup into your five- to ten-gallon bottling bucket before racking in the cider (see p. 21 for siphoning and racking instructions).

This sugar syrup will activate the dormant yeast still alive in your unfiltered and unsulfited cider. With no escape from your capped or corked bottles, the CO_2 from the yeast will be absorbed by the cider, creating the desired sparkling bubbles. After all the sugar is eaten, the yeast will go dormant again. The dormant yeast will leave a bit of sediment at the bottom of the bottle, but don't worry about it. Just be careful not to shake the bottle up, and when you pour your cider, do it at a slow and steady pace without tipping the bottle all the way up. This should keep the yeast in the bottle, as your clear sparkling cider cascades into your glass.

Organizing your bottling area is the key to getting the cider from bottling bucket to the bottles as quickly as possible, thus limiting the harmful effects of air contact. Weather permitting, I prefer to bottle outdoors. A wooden picnic table makes a dandy bottling area, as do sawhorses and an old

wooden door. If bottling inside, clear the kitchen, remove all but one chair and cover the table with a sheet of plastic.

Put the bottles needed in the middle of the table (five gallons fills about fifty-two twelve-ounce bottles or thirty-six sixteen-ounce bottles). At one end of the table, place the capper and caps (still in the saucepan with hot water). Next to this end, either on the bench of the picnic table or on a chair, place an empty bottle carton or case. On the other end of the table, place a plastic milk crate or a similar-sized sturdy box strong enough for a five-gallon container of cider (at least forty pounds) to be placed on top of it.

To get as much clear cider as you can out of every carboy, wait until the carboy is three-fourths drained. Then carefully tilt it toward you while moving the siphon to the bottom corner, just above the lees. With practice you can siphon all but half a bottle from a five-gallon carboy.

Once you have siphoned as much cider as possible out of your carboy, two people should quickly, but carefully, place the bucket of primed cider on top of the box or crate at the end of the bottling table. Once again, get a siphon running, only this time attach your bottle filler to the end of the three-eighths-inch tubing not connected to your racking cane.

The filling tube has a spring-loaded or gravity-feed tip that stops the flow of cider whenever it is lifted off the bottom of the bottle being filled. Holding the bottle filler below the level of the cider, press on the tip until the water in the tubing is replaced by cider (this should be done into a spare bowl or pot). Now you're ready to bottle. Just stick the bottler into a bottle and press down hard enough to let the cider flow.

One person can fill the bottles (no more than three-quarters inch from the top) while another places the caps on top and crimps them. Another can wipe the bottles off and place them back in a case or box. Somebody should probably label your different ciders (you won't remember which is which after a few batches) with either gummed labels or with an indelible, fine-point marker on the bottle cap.

After bottling, clean and sanitize all your equipment, let it air dry, and put it away until another batch needs bottling. Pay special attention to the now empty glass carboy that may have some stubborn smudges where the lees were or around the neck.

Store the capped bottles upright in a dark and quiet area with moderate temperature, about 65 to 72 degrees F (18 to 24 degrees C), so that the yeast may quickly reactivate and carbonate your cider. Corked bottles are stored upright for two weeks, allowing the cork to adhere properly to the inside of the neck. After this, store them on their sides so the corks don't dry out and allow too much air to seep in. Any more than minute amounts of air could cause acetification, eventually turning the cider to vinegar.

Your work is done for now. Just a little more patience is needed while the cider carbonates and recovers from the shock of bottling.

THE REWARDS OF PATIENCE

I start drinking the young cider as soon as it's bottled, often not even waiting for the first bottles to carbonate. The cider is a bit sharp because certain flavors have yet to mellow, but the still unfermented priming sugar takes the edge off. Besides, I like to taste the changes in the cider as it matures and reaches its flavor peak.

The changes that occur during the two- or three-month aging period are very noticeable. Most obvious is that primed cider will become sparkling (within the first month), complementing the cider's natural acidity. More importantly, the cider will mellow as the levels of acids and tannins diminish, exposing more of the richness of the apple taste and extending this to the finish (or aftertaste). The aroma will lose its crispness and develop a slight nuttiness, almost like walnuts. The hues may deepen, especially if adjuncts such as honey or light brown sugar were used.

All cider benefits from aging. The amount of time needed depends on the style of cider you've made. Light ciders may be at their peak as soon as they carbonate and are meant to be drunk while crisp and refreshing. Stronger ciders may take up to three months for all the flavors and alcohol to meld and mellow. Healthy, fully mature cider will remain in peak condition for a year or even two before it slowly starts to decline. Warm storage temperatures, over 70 degrees F (21 degrees C), will accelerate the aging process but shorten the overall life of the cider. Colder temperatures, such as in a refrigerator, are ideal for long-term storage; just remember that the cold inhibits yeast activity, so put the beverages in after they've become sparkling.

All this talk about aging isn't meant to put you off from joyously consuming your nouveau cider. On the contrary, to learn and appreciate the natural process of cidermaking means involvement and observation at each and every step, including smelling and drinking the cider as it evolves.

Finally, after waiting through the fall pressing, winter fermentation, and spring bottling and aging, it is time to bask in the rewards of patience. The fully matured cider, the essence of last year's glorious harvest, is finally ready to drink.

The chilled cider greets you with a ffffffffft when the seal is broken by the opener, and the cap is pulled away from the lip that it has so air-tightly curled around for the last two months. The golden liquid is then poured slowly into a glass as a fountain of foam rises up into the bowl, only to collapse softly onto itself. Shimmering spirals of tiny beaded bubbles rise delicately to the surface of the beverage you created. You raise this symbol of nature's interaction with humanity to your awaiting nostrils, taking in all the freshness and crispness of the apple. Finally, you sip the fruit of your labors and, from here on, you're hooked. Cheers to you, for discovering this tantalizing beverage, and for becoming the latest link to this old and noble tradition.

Troubleshooting

Now remain calm. Potential problems are few and largely preventable. The fact is that cider, with its high acidity and finished alcohol content, is highly resistant to bacterial spoilage and general abuse. Cidermakers don't "burn the contamination midnight oil" as do homebrewers with their bacteria-loving sweet wort (unfermented beer). Anyone familiar with cidermaking and homebrewing can attest to the relatively low incidence of sick cider as opposed to infected beer.

However, don't think for a minute that haphazard methods of production or general sloppiness are without effect, because such practices WILL catch up with you. Spoilage occasionally happens despite close care and the most sanitary surroundings, but losing a batch of cider because of any human error is conduct unbecoming a cidermaster.

Nonbacterial spoilage resulting from contact with certain metals is 100-percent preventable by using the nonreactive plastic, stainless-steel, or glass equipment available today. Do not use funnels, spoons, or any equipment made out of copper or iron, no matter how rustic it may seem. The malic acid in cider reacts with copper, leaving a green tint in your cider, and iron darkens the cider's color considerably. In addition, the cider picks up a metallic taste that prevents anyone from enjoying it. Stick with new equipment and use the five-gallon copper milk jug as an umbrella stand.

Bacterial spoilage is due to notorious "uninvited guests" that get in either because the door was left open or because they were present in the freshly pressed juice and waited for the right conditions to develop. Although many different specific organisms are responsible for souring, stinking up, clouding, or otherwise ruining your cider, they fall into two recognizable groups: acetic acid bacteria and lactic acid bacteria.

Acetic acid bacteria need oxygen to thrive. Thriving for acetobacteria means turning the ethanol in your cider into acetic acid. These bacteria develop into an egg white-like jelly called "the mother" which floats on the surface of the cider and oxidizes it into sharp-tasting cider vinegar. A worthwhile project if vinegar is really what you want to make, but in that case, the vinegar barrel should be located far from your cidery.

To avoid acetification, simply keep air away from the cider. Make sure bungs, corks, and caps fit tightly and water locks are filled to prevent air from seeping in. An area as small as possible should be exposed to air inside a carboy. The cider should be within an inch of the stopper high up in the narrow neck. If thirsty, don't keep nipping at the carboy and exposing more of the surface to the air. Bottle off what you have before you wind up pouring it on salads. Wooden barrels require attention since evaporation (the angels' share) replaces cider with air. Every few weeks the barrel needs to be topped off with fresh cider or sterile water. Acetification is avoidable, so slam the door and keep out the oxygen. If it is too late, enjoy your salads and make sure everything has been sterilized before using your equipment again.

Lactic acid bacteria converts sugars into primarily lactic and acetic acids, CO_2, and glycerol. They are responsible for some of the foulest-smelling and vilest-tasting ciders imaginable (one so bad that the cidermaker, yours truly, was actually proud of the magnitude of the disaster).

Lactic bacteria do not need oxygen to wreak havoc and are resistant to the effects of sterilization. In fact, they are always present in cider and do little harm unless the conditions are right for their development. These conditions include warm temperatures and cider that is low in acid with a high level of unfermented sugars. So make sure your cider doesn't warm up too much during the summer months. Do not use a large percentage of low-acid fruit such as the abundant Red Delicious, but if you do, measure the levels with an acid-testing kit and adjust accordingly. Use yeast that is fresh and vigorous and that ferments out to dryness (the cider may be sweetened at bottling).

It is easier to describe lactic spoilage than it is to figure out which specific bacteria causes it. The first hint of trouble is visual; a very slight translucent haze obscures an otherwise brilliantly clear bottle. Open the bottle, and it may come gushing out or it may pour out in a slimy, oily mess. It will smell like solvent and taste like rotten garbage. Smell and taste it only if you want to recognize the effects, but be forewarned, this is really nasty stuff.

In his studies of wine spoilage, Louis Pasteur gave the different effects of lactic spoilage special names: *la pousse* was the gaseous effect, *la mannite* was the sliminess, and *la tourne* was the stinky rottenness. It was thought that each condition was caused by a different bacteria, but now it is known that many different lactic bacteria can spoil cider in this unpleasant way. There are ways to avoid lactic-spoiled cider, but none that can restore it. By the time it hit my batch of apple/pear cider, there wasn't much I could do except pour it out and sterilize everything it had touched. My mistake was not properly adjusting the acid levels to compensate for the low-acid pears.

In conclusion, the cidermaker should be aware but not intimidated by these risks. You can ferment almost risk free by practicing good sanitation techniques with modern equipment, by using fresh juice and yeast, by keeping the cider cool and away from air, and by adjusting the acid levels to below pH 3.7. Strive to be proud of your accomplishments and not your disasters, no matter how spectacular.

Apples, Juice, & Sugar

You are no longer a rookie cidermaker. You've got at least one season of experience to draw upon and have perhaps one of your own ciders in hand as you ponder more advanced cider techniques and recipes. This section will go beyond store-bought juice to the art of recognizing good cider apples and blending your own juice. Topics including juice treatment, the differences between yeast strains and their effect on finished cider, care and use of wooden casks, and recipes using all kinds of sugars and fruits supply the budding cidermaster with a wide range of information about this exquisite beverage.

Cider is made from apples, but great cider is made from specific apple varieties with superior cider characteristics. Once these varieties are recognized and trac-ked down, cidermakers may avoid the convenient but unknown store-bought fresh pressed sweet ciders. They may instead choose to select their own apples, crush them or have them custom pressed at a cidermill (much easier), and blend them to personal tastes. First of all, cidermakers must know their apples.

APPLE CATEGORIES AND VARIETAL COMPOSITION

Only England and France have significant numbers of true cider apples. Each variety may contain all the elements needed for a well-balanced juice, making blending unnecessary. Frequently, treasured varietal ciders are made using one variety of apple from one specific orchard. For the North-American cidermaker, variety is the spice of life because different apples contribute their characteristics to the blend. Aromatic apples perfume the cider and greet the imbiber. Dessert apples and highacid apples complement each other so that the cider will be well balanced. Astringent apples structure the cider and provide a lingering aftertaste.

AROMATIC
MCINTOSH
APPLES AT
PINE HILL
ORCHARDS

PHOTO BY: CHARLIE OLCHOWSKI

There are four categories of apples, some of which overlap:

• Sweet dessert-type apples have low acid that comprises the bulk of the juice, up to 50 percent of the total. They contain plenty of sugar and their juice is generally light in color. Include at least two varieties in the blend and not too many of the insipid Red Delicious. Varieties include Baldwin, Ben Davis, Cortland, Spartan, Red Delicious, Rome Beauty, York Imperial, and Winter Banana as well as some Golden Delicious strains.

• Medium- to high-acid varieties are both eating and cooking apples whose levels of malic acid give them a certain snappiness and zing. They balance the sweetness of the dessert types and should constitute 30 to 40 percent of the juice. Varieties include Northern Spy, Staymen Winesap, Gravenstein, Jonathan, Granny Smith, Wealthy, Rhode Island Greening, Grimes and Blushing Golden, Yellow Newton, and Pippin.

• Aromatic apples are highly perfumed and contribute to the aroma of the cider. They should make up 10 to 20 percent of the juice. Varieties include McIntosh, Cox's Orange, and Roxbury Russet.

• Astringent varieties are crabapples. These small native fruit are borne on small, often thorny bushes or trees. The apples are extremely high in acid and tannin, and their juice should be used sparingly, no more than 5 percent, to perk up blander juices. The most common species include the American, Southern, Prairie, and Oregon crabapples. (If these are unavailable to you and your cider needs some umph, read about tannin in chapter four, "The Harvest and the Juice.")

Some selected North American apples are further described in the following paragraphs:

• McIntosh is the most popular eating apple. It is medium sized with light green and red markings, glossy, and very juicy. Even though the taste is too plain for any significant contribution, the pronounced sweet aroma of the McIntosh contributes greatly to the cider. This variety is widely available.

• Roxbury Russet was developed before 1654 on the hills

CORTLAND
APPLES AT
PINE HILL
ORCHARDS

PHOTO BY: CHARLIE OLCHOWSKI

of Roxbury above Boston, Massachusetts. It is a medium-sized, very hard apple distinguished by rough, brown skin that is very similar to a Bosc pear. This variety is still considered the finest apple in North America with a balanced taste and exotic aroma. It is very expensive and very limited, so make small quantities of single varietal cider (you'll have to press these yourself) or blend it into a larger batch if you are lucky enough to find some.

BALDWIN APPLES AT PINE HILL ORCHARDS

PHOTO BY: CHARLIE OLCHOWSKI

• Winesap or Staymen Winesap are two widely grown related cultivars with medium acid and a unique winelike tingle. The medium-sized, dusky red fruit are prized as cider apples because their juice perks up otherwise sweet blends, especially those from the Pacific Northwest. This variety is widely available.

• Cortland is a medium to large, round apple with flattened top and bottom. It is a superior apple for applesauce and good for pies. The juice is sweet but not insipid and very pale in color. It has the advantage of oxidizing slowly, keeping the blend from browning. This variety is widely grown in the Northeast.

• Baldwin is another old-time favorite with a popularity in the Northeast which rivals that of the Spy. This variety is a medium-sized, dark red fruit with bluish speckles and a taste as rich as the Spy but less snappy. Baldwins tend to produce heavily every other year, so availability varies.

• Gravenstein is a medium-sized, almost lumpy apple that is either light to medium green or splotched with large areas of red (Red Gravenstein).

It matures early and has a pronounced acid zing. This variety is widely grown in California where it is blended with bland commercial varieties such as Delicious.

• Granny Smith is a cultivar from Australia introduced into the United States rather recently. This variety is well known for its grass-green color and citruslike taste. It is used out west to perk up more sedate blends. It has been grown in the Northeast with mixed results, because the fruit is too often very high in acid and makes the juice taste almost sour.

• Rome Beauty is a big, round, apple-red fruit. It was developed in the Midwest and is

SURPRISINGLY SWEET ROME BEAUTIES AT PINE HILL ORCHARDS

PHOTO BY: CHARLIE OLCHOWSKI

RED DELICIOUS APPLES AT PINE HILL ORCHARDS

PHOTO BY: CHARLIE OLCHOWSKI

sweet but one dimensional. They are used in the base blend because they are cheap and available. They are extremely low in acid with pH up to 4.0 (most apples are in the 3.5 range) and levels of malic acid half to a quarter that of other North American cultivars. If used in any quantity make sure to measure and adjust the sweet cider with high-acid apples or with acid additives.

popular throughout the country. The juice is not outstanding on its own but is very good as a large part of the base blend. It has a very hardy tree whose heavy crops make it widely available at a good price. Interestingly, ciders I have made with a large percentage of Romes tend to leave a bit more residual sweetness in the finished cider, a most pleasant surprise.

• Red Delicious is not a favorite of any cidermaker but one that you will probably use because of its sheer quantity. They are conical, red or dark-red, medium to fairly large apples with pinpoints of white on the shoulders. Look for the five distinctive bumps on the bottom. The flesh is crunchy and

• Northern Spy is a celebrated apple and my favorite for cider. Its usual availability has been somewhat strained by recent popularity. This is what *The American Fruit Book* (John P. Jewett Publisher, 1849), indexing 253 varieties of apples, said about the Spy:

156. Northern Spy. Large; roundish conical; ribbed; smooth, greenish, pale yellow, much dull red, with dark, bright stripes in the sun; stem two thirds of an inch long, rather stout, in a broad, deep cavity; calyx small, nearly closed, in a deep, furrowed basin; flesh yellowish, very tender, juicy, mild, inclining to saccharine, delicious, slightly aromatic. Remarkable for its freshness after long keeping. Winter, Spring, and into Summer. A great, upright grower; good bearer. But it needs a rich soil, high culture, and constant growth, to produce fair fruit, as the tree grows old; and the top must be thinned to expose the fruit to the sun, as it is insipid in the shade. Very hardy in the North, as we find by a few years experience in Maine. This is a new and excellent fruit, and promises to take the place of Roxbury Russet, and many other late kinds of inferior appearance and quality. Origin, farm of

CHERISHED NORTHERN SPIES ON THE TREE AT PINE HILL ORCHARDS

PHOTO BY: CHARLIE OLCHOWSKI

O. Chapin, East Bloomfield, N.Y., from seed from Ct.

This is obviously only a small number of the many apple varieties grown in North America. Apple producing areas may be known for the success of one export, for example Washington State and its Red Delicious, but many cultivars are grown everywhere because locals know their apples and insist on variety. Great cider can be made using locally grown fruit in a balanced blend of the cidermaker's choosing anywhere in North America where there are orchards. Don't wait to go looking for apples late in the season; this is something to do during the "dog days" of summer. Hop in the car, head to the local orchards, and visit the farmstands or cidermills to purchase your apples fresh from the source.

As you grow more experienced, plan to expand your quality control. Familiarize yourself with the well-known varieties grown in your area as well as some of the lesser-known but perhaps more flavorful varieties around. Ask about quality of the fruit because this reflects the influence of weather and the general health of the orchard. Weather affects apples less than other tree fruit because of the long growing season, but a cool and rainy season will produce large fruit with less taste and low sugar levels. On the other hand, a hot dry summer will yield fruit that is smaller and firmer with concentrated sugars and potential for a more robust and trouble-free cider.

The health of an orchard is reflected in its fruit. Notice the differences between apples from a tended orchard and one that isn't. You want to use firm, sound apples in your cider, not bruised, decayed, or soft ones. These may contain mycotoxins, such as patulin, and high levels of bacteria that will infect the rest of your cider. Bargain-priced apples aren't such a bargain if they're bad.

It is important to ask about availability since various apple species bear different yields and often bear them at different times of the season. Gravensteins begin to ripen in August, Russets in October. Baldwins bear heavily every other year, and some, like Romes, are apt to drop their fruit all at once. Finding out from the farmers what varieties are doing well and when they will be picked is the key and first step to choosing your house blend.

Hail damage is localized but intense, scarring the otherwise healthy fruit and preventing them from being sold as premium apples. A similar situation occurs when orchards cut back on their insecticides and sacrifice some blemished fruit for reduced spraying. Scaring and surface blemishes do not affect the taste of the apple or the pressed juice.

Availability is also affected by the renewed interest in apples other than the somewhat bland half dozen or so varieties found in most supermarkets. A few years ago, the prominent grande dame of the American kitchen, Julia Child, started a run on Northern Spys with a most enthusiastic (and entirely warranted) endorsement of this superior apple. The resulting short supply had a long-term silver lining because quite a few growers subsequently grafted less-productive orchards over to Spys.

Ask about apple grades and pricing. In apple country the grades are premium, fancy, or firsts (the top grade). These are unblemished, large apples for retail sales and are generally too expensive for cider.

Seconds are medium- to large-sized apples with surface blemishes and scarring because of insects or weather. These are identical in taste to firsts and often used for desserts, applesauce, etc. They are a good choice for small quantities of superior or rare apples to blend with less expensive ones. The price is almost half that of firsts but still high for a large pressing.

Cider grade is the most flexible category, so quality control is on full alert. Cider-grade apples are not beat up, bruised, or otherwise unworthy of your efforts as cidermaker. Quality cider-grade apples can be downgraded seconds (the result of a large crop), perfect-looking fruits too small for the other categories, or fruits that are very misshapen or scared. A number of rotted fruits deserve attention. Note if the damage seems to be recent from bruises or cuts sustained during harvest or if the whole apple looks rotted from within. Cuts mean that the pickers or packers may have been a little rough — just toss the damaged ones. Whole rotten or moldy apples may be a more serious problem indicating that the apples were laying on the ground for a while before being harvested. Toxins and infections are often transmitted from the soil to the apples and will infect your cider. Steer clear of these drops. Prices for cider-grade apples vary as much as the quality. In ten years of cidermaking, a bushel has cost between three dollars and seven dollars.

CUSTOM PRESSING VERSUS PRESSING YOUR OWN

Getting the sweet cider out of the apples is not as easy as it first may seem. At the presshouse, the apples are washed then ground up in a hammer mill or some other type of grinder. Not all of the astringent pips (seeds) survive this process intact, but their added tang is beneficial to low-tannin dessert apples.

The pulp is then pumped into removable molds lined with nylon to form a stack of apple-filled pillows separated by flat wooden racks measuring between twenty-two and thirty-six inches. For greater juice yield, these racks (now called the cheese) are then pressed slowly with tremendous force by hydraulic presses, some of which operate with 2,200 pounds of pressure per square inch to extract 3 to 3 1/2 gallons of sweet cider per bushel. The pressed sweet cider is then pumped into a refrigerated tank to settle overnight. This allows the solids to fall to the bottom before racking the sweet cider into plastic jugs.

You may crush and press apples at home using a hand-powered or electrically driven apple grinder and press, but I believe these are more expensive than they are worth except for small batches. With yields of only 2 to 2 1/2 gallons per bushel, this method would leave me very sore after grinding and crushing the forty or so bushels of fruit I need for my annual 100-gallon batch. Although people who grow their own apples and crush them are very lucky indeed, it is obvious that most town and city dwellers don't have this luxury. For the folks not able to press the apples of their choice, custom pressing is the best choice and a no-sweat approach to getting the juice out of the fruit.

Custom pressing involves finding a well-run cidermill that presses a variety of apples for its own fresh pressed sweet cider. The house blend is usually composed of the most popular commercial apple varieties such as McIntosh, Red Delicious, Cortlands, Romes, etc. These apples can provide all the aroma and sugar needed to produce great hard cider. Apples from the medium- to high-acid category are all that is required for the ideal blend to be realized.

Now before you go in search of someone to custom press ten gallons of cider for you, here are a few tips:

• There is a minimum amount of cider that can be pressed in one run, usually between thirty and fifty gallons. As stated before, cider is meant to be experienced with others and there is no better excuse for a party than a pressing. Call friends or homebrewers and see if they want to taste some custom pressed sweet cider. Organize a day trip complete with a picnic lunch, apple picking, or foliage tour before picking up the cider at the mill.

• You will have to find and purchase whatever additional apples are needed for your custom blend. Scan the food section of the local papers for orchards that grow the apple varieties you want. Growers know what apples their neighbors have, so the mill owner may suggest a source of specific apples.

• Figure out the total amount of juice you

want pressed and how many additional bushels of apples will be needed. Discuss this with the mill owner or boss and get a rough estimate of the cost and the best time to do the pressing. A quick rule of thumb is that one bushel of apples will give three gallons of juice. A thirty-gallon run, for example, should require about ten bushels of apples. Say the house juice contains a good blend of aromatic and sweet apples but few zippy, medium- to high-acid ones. An ideal balance would be achieved by adding four bushels or so of Spys or Winesaps to six bushels of the mill's assorted cultivars in the crusher.

TOM CLARK SORTS APPLES BEFORE GRINDING THEM AT THE CLARKDALE FRUIT FARMS IN WEST DEERFIELD, MASS.

PHOTO BY: CHARLIE OLCHOWSKI

• The apples need not be brought to the mill the day of the pressing. The additional bushels of apples may be purchased weeks prior to the pressing and kept in the climate-controlled cold rooms at the mill. Most varieties benefit from a week or two of mellowing. The apples are kept out to ripen and soften before pressing. This makes them easier to press and increases the amount of extractable juice.

• Although most mills will rack off the fresh juice into handy one-gallon plastic jugs, it may be easier and less expensive to rack off directly into your five-gallon carboys. Drop them off at the presshouse sanitized and covered. Protect them from accidental breakage by putting them inside plastic milk crates. The crates also make them much easier to move around.

Custom pressing is more involved than just picking up the straight cidermill blend, but the improved quality in the juice as well as the awesome Indian-summer parties that may be had (last year's CiderFest in Westford, Massachusetts, counted sixty

attendees and a 360-gallon custom pressing) more than make up for the extra work. Besides, this is a great way to celebrate the harvest season, the revival of this fantastic beverage, and the inauguration of your first batch of unique custom-pressed cider.

DIFFERENT SUGARS

Sugars are not used solely to boost the specific gravity to the proper level. The sugar's taste will also contribute much to the aroma, color, and flavor of the finished hard cider. Cidermakers are always experimenting, and few are content with only one style of

CRAIG CONSTANTINE FILLS FRAMES WITH CRUSHED APPLES AT PINE HILL ORCHARDS.

PHOTO BY: CHARLIE OLCHOWSKI

CIDER IS EXTRACTED FROM RACK OF APPLE PILLOWS AS ANOTHER RACK WAITS TO BE PRESSED AT THE CLARKDALE FRUIT FARMS.

PHOTO BY: CHARLIE OLCHOWSKI

cider in their cellar. They know that by adding different sugars to each carboy of the same sweet cider they can make as many different hard ciders. The ease with which different ciders are made and fermented is laughable and the envy of the homebrewer.

As always, a specific gravity reading will indicate how much sugar is already in the juice and how much is needed to bring it up to healthy levels (see chapter four, "The Harvest and the Juice"). Next, the sugar or sugars are measured out and may be stirred directly into the carboy or made into a simple syrup for easy mixing. Just heat the sugar in a saucepan with an equal amount of water until dissolved then pour it into the carboy.

The substitution of different sugars will affect the specific gravity to a degree but not enough to worry about. Be aware though that a pound of brown sugar will have a much greater impact on a cider's taste than a pound of corn sugar. Below are some often used sugars:

• Corn sugar is white and very fine grained. It is the choice sugar for brewing beer because of its lack of residual taste. Corn sugar has no use other than to augment low sugars, but it has the ability to dissolve almost instantly.

• Cane sugar is white and medium grained. It is the preferred sugar for adjusting low sugar levels in cider. Cane sugar is inexpensive (stock up during a sale) and available everywhere. Brewers say that cane sugar adds a cidery taste to their beer. Use this if you desire a refreshingly cidery taste in your cider.

• Sucinet is a raw, sugar-cane syrup of medium-brown color. The taste is very different but not unpleasant. Add a small amount to a robust cider. It is available in supply stores.

• Light brown sugar is medium grained. It is a very good sugar to use in hearty New England-style ciders because it is not overpowering if used straight. It imparts a copper color to the cider and a butterscotch aroma (or nose).

• Brown sugar is medium grained, sticky, and strong. It will overpower the taste of any cider if used solely; a ratio of three to one with cane sugar would likely be plenty. It imparts a medium-brown color to the cider.

• Molasses is a thick, dark-colored syrup produced during the refining of sugar or from sorghum. It is not a personal favorite. If you like the taste, use it sparingly. Even a small amount will color the cider.

Note that the addition of honey to cider is discussed in chapter ten under 'Cyser.'

Advanced Fermentation

Running out of hard cider is a tragedy any cidermaker worth his or her weight in apples tries desperately to avoid. This is one reason to increase your production levels now that you have some experience. With lager batches, however, adjustments must be made to ensure a successful fermentation and a quality hard cider. You might try using eight- or fifteen-gallon stainless-steel kegs or wooden barrels instead of five-gallon carboys. Special procedures need to be followed with these vessels to quickly start fermentation and prevent contamination.

If you like the five-gallon batch size, in-creasing overall production gives you the opportunity to experiment with a variety of sugars and yeast strains. One large custom pressing can lead to an array of different hard ciders. You'll have a cider for every mood and every occasion.

This chapter looks at some of the more subtle advantages to increasing your output.

MANY YEASTS OR ONE YEAST

As stated earlier, either wine or beer yeast may be used to ferment cider. Thanks to the explosion in popularity of both home-brewing and home winemaking, an array of new yeast cultures are now available in supply shops. It is not uncommon to face two or even three dozen variations of beer yeast, available in liquid and dried forms. Although this certainly expands our choices, it also thoroughly muddies the waters as to which yeast is the best for cider. One thing I can say for certain — in ten years of tasting hundreds of different ciders I've been amazed at the compatibility of cider to the many different and diverse beer, wine, and wild yeast strains. Each yeast leaves its own imprint on the finished cider, so by using a variety of strains a variety of hard ciders may be made as each ingredient contributes its own flavor profile.

If there is to be one guideline, it should be based on

fermentation temperature. Both lager beer and white wine yeasts are effective at capturing the crispness and acidity of the cider at their ideal temperature range of 45 to 55 degrees F (7 to 13 degrees C). Ale beer yeasts, on the other hand, will retain more of the esters and fruitiness if used at the range of 55 to 65 degrees F (13 to 18 degrees C).

Besides temperature, there is little to inhibit the cidermaker from dividing up the blend into any number of one-, three-, or five-gallon glass jugs and observe their progress as the different yeast strains work at different speeds and create surprisingly different colors. It is only at tasting time that the success of the variety of yeasts can be measured. With luck, you and your cider-drinking friends will be unable to decide on a clear winner, making your variety of ciders a complete success.

There are many cidermakers, however, who have so perfected the taste of their fermented cider that great pains are taken to ensure consistency. Only one or two large batches of cider are made, presenting their own challenges. The primary requirement is to add a large enough amount of active yeast cells to the sweet cider to start fermentation quickly. This blitzkrieg mentality to fermentation ensures that undesirable yeast don't even have time to infect the sweet cider because their numbers are quickly overwhelmed by the rapidly multiplying yeast of choice.

To accomplish this, the cidermaker can purchase the needed amount of yeast from a supply shop. Although very convenient, this may turn out to be rather expensive, especially if one prefers to use high-quality liquid yeast cultures. A very satisfactory alternative is step culturing. This involves pitching the yeast into a sterilized bottle, one-third filled with boiled and cooled sweet cider. Within a few days the mini-fermenter is in full swing. Then pitch the contents into a larger mini-fermenter and so on until a sufficient amount of active yeast starter (between 2 and 5 percent of the total amount being fermented) may be pitched into the waiting carboy or other large container

STEP CULTURING

Step culturing increases the quantity of active yeast you add to your large container of sweet cider, thus ensuring a quick and successful fermentation. A step culture is produced by adding a small amount of yeast to a small quantity of sweet cider in a sanitized environment. After the yeast feed on the sugars in the sweet cider and multiply, pour them into a larger container of fresh sweet cider. This process is repeated until a large enough colony of yeast is ready to go to work on you cider.

Be aware that the chances for contamination rise as cultures are exposed to air and pitched from one container to another. However, by following strict standards you will be able to inoculate your large vat of cider with top-quality yeast at little cost. The benefits of step culturing far outweigh the risks of contamination.

Here is a list of items you will need for step culturing:

• a plastic or stainless-steel funnel
• a strong sanitizing solution of one tablespoon bleach per gallon of water
• a large beer bottle (at least twenty-two ounces) and a bottle cap
• a bored rubber stopper to fit the bottle
• a water lock
• about one cup of fresh pressed sweet cider
• one inflated package of liquid beer or wine yeast, ready to pitch

1. Prepare sanitizing solution and soak the funnel, the rubber stopper, and the water lock. Cover the bottle with water in a kettle and boil for fifteen minutes.

2. Bring the cider to a boil in a saucepan. Lower the heat and simmer for ten minutes.

3. Boil the single bottle cap for five minutes in water. Cover and remove from heat.

4. Remove the funnel from the solution. Air dry.

5. Drain the hot water from the bottle and, using the funnel to prevent spills, pour the boiled juice into the bottle. Cap immediately. Rinse the funnel well and return it to the solution.

6. Let the boiled sweet cider cool to room temperature. Remove the funnel, rubber stopper, and water lock from the solution and rinse off. Remove the cap from the bottle, swab the inflated foil yeast pack with the sanitizing solution, cut it open, and use the funnel to pour it directly into the cooled sweet cider. Place the bored stopper and water lock on immediately.

NEW ENGLAND CIDERMAKER RICK SMITH AND HIS WOOD BARRELS FULL OF CIDER

PHOTO BY: CHARLIE OLCHOWSKI

7. Set the bottle at room temperature. Within a day some activity will be observed. Within two or three days, the yeast will be at its peak of activity. At this point, the active yeast culture is ready to be pitched into a larger container up to twice its size. Follow the same instructions as above.

Ideally, a yeast starter should be 5 percent of the amount that you want fermented. At this rate, signs of fermentation can be observed in a matter of hours. In reality, we make due satisfactorily with much less, as little as 2 percent. The risk of contamination is higher since it takes the yeast longer to get started, but so far, a visible fermentation within two or three days seems to work out just fine.

LARGE-CONTAINER FERMENTATION

To avoid the tragedy of running out of cider, one must usually increase the amount of cider produced from one year to the next. As your skills increase, the demands for your interpretation of what cider is will also increase. Most cidermakers I know make between thirty and fifty gallons a year for their families and friends, not an excessive annual amount. To accommodate this and larger quantities, the modern cidermaker will ferment the bulk of the cider in stainless steel barrels, not in wooden casks.

Okay, I know that wooden casks filled with your own cider are about as cool a sight as you'll ever see, at least in your own basement. But the fact is, they make lousy fermenters. Besides being expensive (about 125 dollars for a fifteen-gallon barrel), new casks cannot be used to ferment cider anyway because the new wood is too harsh, even to ferment something as sturdy as red grapes for wine. Rather, the showy oak barrels are used to finish strong ciders prior to bottling. The brief contact with wood imparts a unique aroma and vanilla-like finish. This is covered in greater detail in chapter ten, under 'New England-style Cider.'

Used oak barrels present problems of their own. I strongly advise against using them unless you know for sure that the barrel is oak and has never held anything but cider or white wine, the staves and hoops are strong and secure, and the porous wood has never been contaminated with molds or bacteria. In other words, if these criteria aren't met, and you are set on using an oak cask, take the plunge and invest in a new oak barrel. Even though it will only be good to finish strong cider at first, in the long run it will be worth the expense.

Okay now, let's assume that you are lucky enough to have or been given a properly used barrel (I have!), or been driven enough to plop down $125 for a new one (I have!). To err on the side of caution you should treat both used and new oak barrels the same way: with rigorous cleaning. This cleaning will reduce the harsh tannins in the wood, tighten up the staves to make the barrel leakproof, and reach into the wood to eliminate harmful bacteria or yeasts.

First, steam clean the barrel. Industrial-type steam cleaners can be rented or, better still, go to your friendly corner garage and see if they can do it for you. The promise of a few bottles of nature's finest is usually all it takes. Put the nozzle into the barrel and let it steam away until the water runs out clear. This steam leaches out the excessive woody taste.

If the steam option is unavailable to you, chemicals may be used to leach out the tannins. "Barrelkleen," or some other brand name, should be available in homebrew/wine-maker supply stores. Follow the instructions included with whatever chemical you choose.

Once the tannins are subdued, rinse the barrel with clean water. Then fill the barrel with clean water and add two tablespoons of plain, unscented household bleach for every five gallons of water. Bung the barrel and let it sit overnight. This inexpensive solution will sanitize the insides and swell the wood to make it tight.

Drain your barrel, and it is now ready to fill with cider. If you are not going to use it right away, you will need to fill it with a solution of potassium metabisulphite because a wooden barrel will dry out and eventually fall apart if not tended properly. For every five gallons of water, dissolve one ounce potassium metabisulphite crystals (powdered Campden tablets) and one-half ounce citric acid crystals. Fill the barrel with this and keep it bunged up tight. Drain and replace with fresh solution every two months or so.

Stainless-steel barrels or kegs are used by beer companies for their draft beer. The most common is the half barrel, which holds 15 1/2 gallons; keep your eyes open for the nifty quarter barrels of 7 3/4 gallons. Stainless-steel kegs are nonporous, easy to clean, and almost beyond breaking, a most perfect vessel for the cidermaker's preferred house cider. Smaller quantities of other styles may be made in regular five-gallon glass carboys. Used kegs can be bought from beer distributors or from flea markets, and deals can be made on those that have been banged around a bit. Make sure they have been depressurized before you use them. Expect to pay between ten dollars and twenty dollars for a used keg.

Kegs have one bunghole, a screw-in pressure valve on one side, and a dispenser valve on the head. The valves can be removed by placing a screwdriver in the groove, grasping it with pliers, and turning the whole valve counterclockwise. These should be taken apart and thoroughly sanitized before being put back into place.

Use a penlight and peer inside the keg through the bunghole. Remember that grunge and filth are easily removed with a high-pressure hot water spray (your local garage can help you out) and a carboy brush. Sanitizing is done with either a bleach solution or B-Brite. What you are looking for are signs that the stainless steel is pitted, the valve gaskets don't seal, or the bunghole is damaged in such a way that a rubber-bored stopper (number 11) cannot be properly fitted. Before you fill the fifteen-gallon keg (or any larger fermenter for that matter) with fresh cider, be certain that it is out of the way and high enough off the ground so the contents can be racked off into a container below it. Sturdy basement worktables are ideal keg racks. They are strong enough to support the weight and provide plenty of room underneath for all the cidermaking gear. Small dowels or wooden wedges should be affixed to the table top to secure the kegs and prevent them from rolling.

First put the sugar or other adjuncts (if they are part of the recipe) in the keg, then pour in gallon jugs of fresh sweet cider into the keg through a sanitized funnel placed in the bunghole. Fill to the top of the barrel, just below the bunghole, and carry on with the recipe.

KEGGING

You would be hard pressed to find a fermentable liquid as versatile as cider. The high acidity, light color, and rich taste make cider very adaptable to stylistic changes. All the cidermaker has to do is vary the yeast and/or the adjuncts. These attributes also make the cider itself an excellent base for all kinds of experimentation. The addition of honey, fruits, and spices results in a variety of beverages too numerous to list. Be bold with your cidermaking. (The recipes starting on p. 43 are some of the more successful variations and should be considered as an incentive to the daring.) Let your only rules be quality ingredients and good sanitation; anything else is open to fermentation.

Collecting empties and washing them all at the end of a party can be a real drag on the post-party glow. Many cidermakers avoid this hassle by kegging a portion of their stock in three- or five-gallon stainless steel containers known as Cornelius kegs. These are normally used to dispense soda under pressure but they are ideal for partytime situations.

The valves on Cornelius kegs should be taken apart, cleaned, and sanitized, just like the valves on the larger stainless-steel barrels. Check the gaskets for wear and replace if needed. Clean and sanitize the inside following the procedure outlined on p. 40. Once cleaned initially, Cornelius kegs are a snap to maintain and are almost indestructible. They also have the distinct advantage of being light enough to carry around when full and small enough to fit in a refrigerator for a chill.

The one disadvantage of having the full kegging system is cost. Valves, hoses, and a CO_2 canister are part of the package that pressurizes and dispenses your cider from a tap. A kegging system can be the highest ticket item in your cidery but one that is well worth it. You should be able to find a Cornelius set up at soda-bottling companies and distributors as well as your local homebrew supply store. Deals may also be found by perusing the ads in the back of homebrew magazines, but beware of the shipping costs.

When fermentation is complete, siphon the finished and cleared cider from the glass carboys into a sanitized Cornelius (or any other type) stainless-steel keg. To carbonate a five-gallon keg, add a priming syrup made by boiling together one-half cup (no more than that) cane or corn sugar and two cups water. Fill the keg completely to the top to minimize the ullage (airspace) and seal tightly to prevent airborne bacteria from reaching the cider and very possibly turning it to cider vinegar. Store the cider upright in a cool place to mellow and age for a few months. During this time the cider will carbonate. The dormant yeast cells will be activated by the new food source and will convert the sugar syrup to bubbles and a wee bit more alcohol, leaving a small amount of sediment in the keg.

A few days before you are ready to tap the keg, place it in the refrigerator to chill. To remove the unsightly but harmless sediment before moving the keg, attach the hoses and let the cider flow until it is clear. You will only lose a few glasses, well worth the eye-pleasing clarity.

Remember that once a keg is tapped, it must be consumed quickly since the space occupied by the cider is replaced with air. This perishability along with the ease of post-party clean-up makes kegged cider the beverage of choice for large events. These gatherings, from ciderfests to pig roasts, are an important part of the cidermasters busy year-round social calendar.

But what if people are clamoring for your cider at this weekend's party and you don't even have it out of the fermenters yet? No need to panic if you have the kegging system complete with a CO_2 canister and quick-connect hoses. This system pressurizes the keg and pushes the cider out through the tap the same way a soda dispenser serves carbonated soft drinks. If your cider is fermented and cleared, you can keg and be ready to serve your nouveau cider almost as soon as the occasion arises.

Whatever size fermenter you decide to siphon from, remember again that all cider must be quickly protected from air. For this reason, choose the fermenter closest in size to the amount you are kegging. Follow all sanitary procedures as you quietly rack the new cider from the fermenter to the waiting keg. Be aware that the newly kegged cider has not undergone extended aging and may still be a bit sharp in taste. This is expertly remedied by adding a sweetener of some kind to the cider in the keg. A sweetening syrup (two parts water to one part sugar, boiled and cooled) may be stirred in, as well as frozen apple juice concentrate, corn syrup, honey, or even a flavored syrup such as raspberry or menthe. Whatever you use, sweeten to taste by gently adding and stirring until you decide it's sweet enough.

Tightly seal your keg of nouveau cider and put it on ice or in the refrigerator to chill. To serve, simply attach the hoses and pressurize the keg with the CO_2 to the manufacturers specifications (usually five pounds) to start the flow of cider to the appreciative crowd.

BEWARE: This "cider in a hurry" is to be consumed within three or four days. It takes only one-half cup of sugar to properly carbonate and pressurize a five-gallon keg, much more is needed to sweeten it. If the yeast still present in the cider is allowed time to consume all or part of the large quantity of added sugars, the resulting buildup of CO_2 inside the keg could become excessive. At the least, the cider would gush out like a shaken soda, at the worst, you could launch cider torpedoes!

Recipes

The following are some of my favorite recipes for various styles of hard cider. These recipes are guidelines for you to use, but don't be afraid to make changes or adjustments to suit your own tastes (especially with the spices). Keep in mind these recipes are not all for five-gallon batches. You may need pick up equipment to match your larger ambitions.

RASPBERRY CIDER

Raspberries have always held a special place in the cellars and casks of cidermakers. Their vibrant color, heady perfume, and exotic taste coupled with their fragility make them the most prized of the berry fruits used in fermenting. Note that cider and raspberry seasons do not coincide, so you may want to prepare your own raspberries by placing the unwashed berries on a cookie sheet and freezing them in single layers before storing them in freezer-proof bags or plastic containers. Store-bought frozen raspberries are fine as long as they are plain berries and not frozen in heavy syrup.

You will be fermenting the cider in stages; a few weeks after the beginning of the primary stage, the raspberries will be added to the fermenter to contribute their qualities to the cider. At the end of this period, when fermentation slows, only the cider is siphoned off into a clean carboy to continue a quieter secondary fermentation. After the addition and subsequent separation of the berries from the cider, the process for this recipe is the same as any other cider. What is really not the same is the popularity of Raspberry Cider. You would be wise to make plenty because demand usually outstrips supply.

Ingredients for five gallons:

5 gallons fresh pressed sweet cider
5 cups cane or corn sugar
   beer yeast starter (ale or lager)
3 pounds raspberries (defrosted if
   previously frozen)

Pour the sweet cider into a seven-gallon plastic fermenting bucket or a seven-gallon carboy. Measure the sugars and acids and adjust if needed. Dissolve the sugar in five cups boiling water before cooling and add to the juice. Pitch the yeast, seal the plastic or glass fermenter tightly with a bored-rubber stopper, and fit with a water lock.

In a few days, the yeast will begin consuming the sugars in the sweet cider and primary fermentation will start. After two or three weeks, the fermentation will subside somewhat, so at this point add the berries to the fermenting cider. Experience has shown that adding the berries after the vigorous first part of the fermentation helps contain the intense raspberry aromas. Put the tight-fitting stopper and water lock back on the fermenter, or if using a plastic container, just replace the airtight lid and fermentation lock and sit back for a few weeks as the yeast extracts the color and flavor from the berries.

The addition of the berries will energize the fermentation, but after another two or three weeks, the raspberries will look pretty disgusting. The cider will be a cloudy-pink color and most of the tan, slimy-looking berries will be floating on top, buoyed by CO_2 bubbles. Don't worry about their appearance, they gave their flavor and color to your cider, the supreme sacrifice.

Once this extract has been achieved and the berries have nothing more to contribute, the cider must be racked so that it can clear. This is done with the normal equipment used for racking with a small addition: a small piece of fine plastic screening over one end of the siphoning tube to prevent the berries from being sucked up. To do this, grab the end of the siphoning tube that will be immersed into the fermenter.

Loosely fit the small (three square inches or so) sanitized patch of fine plastic screening around the open end and gather it tightly around the tube with a sanitized tie-wrap. You do not want the screening flush with the tube opening but almost "shower-capped" over the opening and secured. This should prevent any berries from getting sucked in. Remember to place the screened end into the full fermenter.

Place the new carboy below the full carboy or bucket and using either mouth suction or the water siphon technique (see p. 21) start the flow of still-fermenting Raspberry Cider gently into the bottom of the second carboy. There will be a good amount of sediment and muck on the bottom of your fermenter. Avoid the urge to get every last drop into your secondary fermenter because you are trying to leave the muck behind. Top off your new fermenter with fresh cider, attach a water lock, and let the young cider (at this point only six to eight weeks old) alone while it continues to ferment.

In another four to six weeks, the cider should be fully fermented, although a few bubbles may still rise to the top. As fermentation slows, the cider will clear and the color deepen as the solids fall to the bottom of the fermenter. If this doesn't happen, carefully move the cider to a cool or downright cold spot for a few weeks to hasten the process. When the cider is clear and the color is vibrant (put a flashlight against the carboy to check), it's ready to bottle.

Raspberry Cider is outstanding and deserves to be showcased. The color is stunning, the aroma is intoxicating, and the taste captures the intensity of the berries against the richness of the apples. For these reasons, I recommend that the Raspberry Cider be bottled off in the following ways:

• Sparkling Raspberry Cider is the ultimate festive beverage. Siphon off the finished cider and stir in a sugar syrup containing one-half cup sugar and one cup water boiled together and cooled to prime. Bottle off in heavy champagne bottles and cap or, better still, use plastic stoppers and wire down. Let these carbonate and age for at least eight weeks before enjoying, at brunch perhaps.

• Cork-finished cider is as elegant as it gets. Siphon the still, unprimed cider directly off into clear glass wine bottles (available in either 375-milliliter or 750-milliliter size at winemaking supply stores). Drive in the corks and remember to let the bottles sit upright for two weeks to set before placing them on their sides. Let it age for at least eight weeks. Keep these bottles protected from all light because the uncolored glass offers no protection from the harmful effects of electric or natural light.

CHERRY CIDER

In place of raspberries, the same quantity of cherries may be fermented with cider. Since cherries ripen earlier than apples, the frugal cidermaker may purchase and freeze the fruits in the middle of the season when quality is high and prices are low. Follow the same procedures as for Raspberry Cider, but remove the stems and pit the cherries before tossing them into the fermenter. This prevents a real mess of solids in the bucket and opens up the tougher-skinned cherries to the yeast.

Cherry Cider is a beautiful true cherry-red color (if you use Bings) with an almost overpowering fragrance. It is rich in taste and finishes cherry tart. Try serving it with cherries jubilee over ice cream for an unforgettable dessert.

GABRIEL'S CRANBERRY CIDER

If you are lucky enough to live in one of the cranberry-producing areas of the country, then you're probably already familiar with the unique bitter and tart flavor that makes the cranberry so special. If not, you've probably tasted the cause of the cranberry industry's recent financial boom: that wonderful product of cranberry and apple juices. It's a match made in heaven. I know you'll enjoy the beautiful garnet color and the wonderful blend of tastes and smells that come from this remarkable union.

The acidity in cranberry juice, while well matched by its astringency (not unlike that produced by high-tannin cider apples), needs to be balanced by sweetness in the finished cider. For that reason, this cider should be sweeter than most others in this book. The final gravity should be 1.010.

To ensure residual sweetness, I use Campden tablets (sodium metabisulfite, available in homebrew stores). There is a controversy surrounding sulfite use, so I'll take a moment to explain. (An alternate without sulfites follows, in which minor changes should produce a final result nearly as good.) Sulfites stop the reproductive processes of many types of microorganisms. What is most important to us is their effect on yeast and bacteria. Tiny quantities of sulfite are very effective at inhibiting bacterial growth, which is great since acetic and lactic bacteria are the nemeses of any cidermaker. Sulfite inhibits some yeast forms, far less than it does other microbes, allowing such yeast to propagate and take over the cider. Sulfites also slow down the rate of fermentation, an absolute necessity for sweeter ciders.

Do not use champagne yeast in this cider. Such yeast are notoriously voracious eaters and will devour all the available sugars in the cider, rendering it much too dry for this recipe.

Ingredients for five gallons:

> **4 1/2 gallons of sweet cider**
> **sugar to bring the specific gravity**
> **up to 1.065**
> **10 twelve-ounce bags of cranberries**
> **(7 1/2 pounds or 100 ounces of juice)**
> **Campden tablets (optional)**
> **1 teaspoon tannin powder**

Pour the sweet cider into your primary fermenter, with enough sugar to raise the specific gravity to 1.065. Add five crushed Campden tablets. If no bittersweet cider apples went into your sweet cider and it lacks bite, add one teaspoon tannin powder (see p. 15). Then put a fermentation lock on and wait for the wild yeast to start going.

While you are waiting, you need to take those cranberries and juice them. It may be easier to do this in stages, bit by bit, but here's the basic idea. Put the cranberries in a pot with enough water to just about cover them and bring the water to a boil. Reduce heat but keep the pot simmering. Soon the cranberries will swell up, pop open, and become soft enough to squeeze. Before you attempt to squeeze the berries, let them cool down. Squeeze the juice through a sanitized cheese cloth (boiled in water for ten minutes) and add the juice to the fermenting cider. Two or three cups of sugar should be added to correct the specific gravity, since cranberries have very little sugar of their own.

Now your cran-apple cider is starting to go. As always, try to avoid foam getting into the airlock. After a couple of weeks, or when a significant layer of sediment has built up, rack the cider into another clean sanitized carboy. Top off with cider or boiled water. Racking the cider at this point calms down the fermentation. It should be kept in a cool room now, approximately 50 degrees F (10 degrees C).

When the sediment has built up and the specific gravity has dropped to around 1.015 or 1.020, rack your cider again. At this point, you want to stop the fermentation and let the cider clear, so add five more Campden tablets (or one per gallon). This is necessary because the original tablets have nearly evaporated by now. In less than a month, your cider should be crystal clear. Test it by shining a flashlight through it. When it's clear, bottle per instructions for basic cider. Don't worry, the sulfites will nearly all have evaporated by bottling time, so your cider will have developed a nice sparkle in the bottle, and no trace of sulfur will remain in the taste. In a few months,

when you pour out your first glass, the bubbles will look enchanting as they rise through the deep-red nectar you've created.

The alternate method is simple. To start the cider, either add a prepared yeast culture or step culture a yeast sample to add on your own (see p. 38). Or if you're feeling adventurous, just see what the wild yeast in your cider will produce on their own. Either way, the cider should start fermenting in several days. After the foam has fallen, when the specific gravity has dropped to around 1.035, rack your cider carefully and place it in a cold cellar, no warmer than 55 degrees F (13 degrees C). Rack it every few weeks or whenever a significant amount of sediment has built up. Continue this until it has stopped fermenting and your cider is crystal clear. What you're actually doing is putting the yeast slowly to sleep in the colder temperatures, causing them to fall to the bottom of the carboy. Then it's like stealing candy from a sleeping baby. You just whisk the cider away, leaving less and less yeast in the cider each time. This process slows down fermentation further. It takes some skill to get this just right. The most important things are low temperature, a good racking (don't stir up that sediment), and a cooperative yeast – some will refuse to be lulled to sleep.

PEAR/APPLE CIDER

Cider made exclusively with pears is called perry and has proven to be less exciting and successful than using an apple/pear blend. Pears have a more subtle taste that is somewhat lost during fermentation and they are not nearly as acidic as apples. Without the acid zing, straight perry tastes thin and lacks the defense against lactic bacteria infection that high acid levels provide. This does not mean the noble pear is of no use to the cidermaker. *Au contraire*, the subtleties of the pear blends well with the apple, creating a beverage that is refined and elegant.

The culture of pears is similar to that of apples, so you should have no trouble finding them in apple country. Having a small amount custom pressed may take some searching, so it may be easier for a group of friends to get together and split up a small thirty- or fifty-gallon, custom-pressed batch of 50/50 apple/pear juice.

Varieties of pears are not as numerous as those of apples. The most common pears grown are the Anjou, the Red Anjou, the russet-skinned Bosc, and, in the Northeast, the very sweet Seckel or Honey pear. Use two varieties for the best balance.

The apple portion of the juice should be composed of at least three varieties in a good orchard blend.

Ingredients for five gallons:

> **5 gallons of sweet apple cider and**
> **pear juice (50/50 blend)**
> **5 cups cane or corn sugar**
> **acid blend and tannin powder**
> **liquid lager beer yeast or dried**
> **white wine yeast**

The addition of so much pear juice will weaken the apple juice, so it is important that the blend be accurately measured and adjusted. Sugar and especially acid levels will need to be boosted. Add sugar accordingly and add acid blend (available in winemaking supply stores) at the rate recommended on the package. The addition of one teaspoon of tannin powder will also strengthen the juice as well as give it some structure for the finish.

The suggested yeasts were chosen for their clean fermentation and dry finish. These traits help accentuate the distinguished aroma and flavor profile of the pears while downplaying the robustness of the apples. Fermentation should proceed as outlined in a sanitized glass or stainless-steel container at the cool temperatures recommended for white wine or lager yeast, 50 to 65 degrees F (10 to 18 degrees C).

Clearing will be gradual, and your apple perry may never be as brilliantly clear as cider, but the very slight haze will hardly be noticeable.

Perry/apple cider can be finished still, but the rising bubbles in sparkling perry really enhance the delicate pear aroma.

PEACHY-KEEN CIDER

This fantastic late-summer Peachy-Keen Cider was the result of a fruit grower's ingenuity when faced with the least preventable of problems to befall an orchard: a fast-moving thunderstorm accompanied by hail.

The Trask family in Dunstable, Massachusetts, had a hilltop peach and apple orchard that was hit hard by small-sized hail that pockmarked the hard and immature peaches and apples. These fruits ripened fine; rot and disease did not set in because of the very dry conditions during the summer. However, the fruit was rated utility grade because of its scarred and rough skin (this grading has only to do with size and appearance, not taste). Faced with too many good fruits that would have otherwise gone unsold, both peaches and apples went into the crusher that season, much to the delight of area sweet- and hard-cider drinkers.

The apples that were included at about a 50/50 ratio were early crop varieties, moderate in sugar but zesty from fairly high amounts of acid. In fact, this worked very well to balance the low acid but very sweet and fragrant peaches.

This is a great summer cider, as aromatic as any with a blend of tastes so good that cidermakers shouldn't wait until misfortune strikes a hard-working fruit producer. So delay those rain and hail dances because I've included an alternative recipe that uses peach juice concentrate.

Ingredients for ten gallons:

> **10 gallons of sweet apple cider and**
> **peach juice (50/50 blend)**

sugar to bring the specific gravity
up to at least 1.065
2 teaspoons tannin powder
lager beer yeast culture

Take a specific gravity reading of the juice. As previously mentioned, the combination of fruits is not very specific, so determine the gravity and add sugar accordingly. Remember that one cup of sugar per gallon of juice will raise the specific gravity about 20 points (see p. 15 for more information).

The tannin powder is added to compensate for the lack of tannin in the peaches, and I find that lager beer yeast at a cool temperature work well to preserve the peachy aromas and tastes.

Ferment the Peachy-Keen Cider following the standard methods with the exception of racking. The peaches have a heavy sediment, so racking the cider after primary fermentation is advised. Just wait until the bubbling in the water lock has slowed down and only smaller bubbles continue to rise through the murky new cider. Then quietly rack the cider off the lees into two sanitized five-gallon carboys. Top them off with fresh apple cider before putting the locks back on.

Peachy-Keen Cider is at its best when sparkling, so prime it with a sugar syrup of one cup of sugar boiled and cooled with two cups of water (this is for ten gallons) before bottling.

PEACHY-KEEN CIDER WITH PEACH JUICE CONCENTRATE

Peach juice concentrate is available in winemaking and homebrew supply stores and is usually used to make peach wine. It is also a very worthy substitute for fresh (but usually unobtainable) peach juice. Packing sizes vary although the nearly four-pound can seems to be the most common. You will need

an amount that will equal four or five gallons when reconstituted, so read the back label or ask a salesperson at the shop.

Keep in mind that the directions for reconstitution will call for the addition of water and sugar to bring the juice up to winemaking specifications. This means that the specific gravity will be high, somewhere around 1.095. Taking readings is critical, because the cidermaker must blend the peach juice concentrate with an amount of fresh sweet apple cider to equal ten gallons, while making sure that the specific gravity is at least 1.065. Hold off adding any sugar until the juices are blended and an accurate reading can be made.

After the juice is blended and measured, add the tannin powder and proceed as the previous recipe indicates.

NEW ENGLAND-STYLE CIDER

This is the infamous hard cider of the colonies, rich in flavor and high in alcohol, long lived, and the bane of the early prohibitionists. Care must be taken, and sanitation must be of the highest order since this cider is turned by wild yeasts. Although risky, these yeast strains give a complexity and depth to the finished cider unmatched by any commercial yeasts. If the thought of unknown guests flourishing in your sweet cider frightens you, a robust Epernay champagne yeast will do the trick.

This is a rich, flavorful cider of the highest quality. Ingredients and production techniques for this cider have changed little over the last 300 years. The one concession to progress is the use of stainless steel or glass as a fermenter and not the traditional wooden barrel. Traditionalists will scoff, and rightly so, as I can also personally attest to having had great barrel-fermented ciders. I can also attest to the many vinegary, cloudy, and otherwise vile offerings that I've politely accepted out of the ol' barrel.

However badly I speak of wooden barrels as fermenters, I can highly recommend the use of new oak casks (if you're lucky to have them) or convenient oak chips as a finishing touch on a robust cider such as this. The wood rounds out the edges and adds another layer of vanilla-like aromas and complex tastes to an already aromatic and flavorful cider. (Because the oak can add so much to this cider, a section on how to properly use your oak cask or chips is included in this recipe.)

Ingredients for fifteen gallons:

> **15 gallons fresh pressed sweet cider (you'll use a bit less)**
> **15 cups any combination of cane, corn, or light-brown sugar with no more than 3 cups of brown sugar or 1 cup of molasses**
> **1 tablespoon tannin powder**
> **2 pounds naturally dried raisins**

Make sure your keg is secure and high enough off the ground that cider may be easily siphoned from it. Fifteen gallons of cider is more than you want to move around.

Using a funnel, pour the sugars and the tannin powder into the sanitized keg, then pour in the cider until it comes up to the bottom of the bunghole. Cover the bunghole with plastic wrap to keep insects out and wait a week or so for the wild yeast to kick in. These yeast are the companion yeast in the orchard and get into the juice on the apple. They are the whitish film on the skin called the bloom (it is not spray residue).

Once wild fermentation gets going, the cidermaker must wipe down the keg and counters daily with sanitizing solution, because the cider goes crazy (wild yeast are voracious eaters) and rids itself of solids. The barrel will also have to be topped off almost daily with fresh cider.

In two or three weeks, primary fermentation will slow to a steady, hissing bubble without foam since the cider has already cleansed itself somewhat. At this point, add the raisins to the keg (you may have to siphon out a bit of cider to make room), wipe down the bunghole area, and put in a number 11 bored-rubber stopper and attach a fermentation lock filled with a light bleach solution. The addition of the raisins may cause the cider to foam up through the water lock. If this happens, just put your finger tightly on top of the lock to prevent it from draining back into the barrel and remove it. Sanitize the area around the bunghole, the stopper, and the water lock before putting it back in place with fresh sanitizing solution.

Raisins contribute sugars, wild grape yeasts, and tannins to the cider, as well as the element of authenticity to the style. In time, they will plump up and gather at the top of the barrel. Do not be alarmed by how they will look floating on top all covered with brown gunk (spent yeast). Looks aren't everything. By early winter, twelve to sixteen weeks after getting this cider started, fermentation will be complete, and the cider will slowly clear. Don't rack this cider: let it stay on its lees until bottling time, unless you plan to finish your cider with oak.

New England-style Cider is robust and complex and takes well to oak finishing. Tie a sanitized piece of screen over the opening of the siphoning tube (see the Raspberry Cider recipe, p. 43) to prevent raisins from clogging it, then siphon the dry and brilliantly clear cider off the lees (be careful to keep the tube off the bottom) and into a fifteen-gallon sanitized new oak cask or into another sanitized stainless steel keg. Remember that the oak cask or the stainless-steel keg will have to be hoisted off the ground, so be prepared to siphon into a sanitized bucket and carefully pour into the awaiting cask or keg. Top off the oak barrel with a similar fermented cider or boiled and cooled water and bung the cask up tight. The new oak will impart its qualities to the cider so quickly that the cider should be tasted after five days and every day thereafter until the desired level is attained, usually between a week and ten days.

If using oak chips to impart the traditional aromas and tastes, place about one-half pound of chips in a cheesecloth or grain bag (both available in homebrew or winemaking stores) and boil in water for about five minutes to sanitize. Place the bag into the keg and siphon in the cider. Top off, bung up tightly, and let it sit for between one and two weeks.

At the end of the oak finishing, the cider may be racked directly into bottles and capped or corked for still cider. Or a simple syrup, containing 1 1/2 cups sugar and one quart of water, may be stirred in before capping for sparkling cider. In two months, the components will have come together. If the stash lasts longer, the cidermaker will have created a true gustatory masterpiece: a deep gold hard cider with complex and varied aromas, a rich, layered taste, and a long and drying finish ... what a mouthful! As good now as it was in Revolutionary times.

BILL'S BASIC BARREL CIDER

Bill Slack really gets into his avocations. He is in the upper hierarchy of two brewing clubs (New Hampshire's Brew Free or Die and Boston's Wort Processors), he is a super cook (his tea-smoked duckling is fabulous), and he turns out a dynamite New England-style cider. Bill patiently waits for the season's last pressing, because he knows it includes rich-tasting, late-ripening varieties such as Northern Spy, Baldwin, and the Holy Grail of American apples, the Roxbury Russett.

Methods of fermentation are traditional, and wild yeast are used to turn the juice. Patience is needed, since it takes a while for the rich tastes to blend. But the finished cider has a fabulous earthy fragrance, deep golden color, and a taste that is both refined and wild.

Ingredients for five gallons:

> **5 gallons late-season, fresh pressed sweet cider**
> **2 1/2 cups cane sugar**
> **2 1/2 cups light brown sugar**
> **1 cup natural (unsulfured) raisins**

Before adding any sugar, take a hydrometer reading of the juice. If it is between 1.040 and 1.045, an additional one-half cup of each sugar will be needed. If it is above 1.045, proceed with the stated amounts. Pour the sugars into a clean and sanitized five-gallon carboy and simply pour the juice in after them until it comes up to the neck of the carboy. Tie a piece of gauze or cheesecloth over the opening to keep out unwanted guests and bugs, and wait for the wild yeast that are already in your juice to start working. At 60 degrees F (16 degrees C) or so, this could take anywhere from two days to a week.

When primary fermentation begins in earnest, remove the gauze and tie a clean towel around the neck of the carboy to absorb any foam or liquid that comes up over the top and down the neck. Remove this towel daily and rinse in a sanitizing bleach solution. It may be used to wipe up any spills as well.

In a few weeks, when the primary fermentation subsides, top off the carboy and attach a fermentation lock. Let the cider continue to work until you can see sediment starting to cake on the bottom of the carboy. At this point, add the raisins and check daily. The fermentation may start up a bit because of the addition of the raisins (the cider may bubble up through the water lock, in which case it should be washed and new sanitizing solution added before being put back on).

After a few days when you are certain that the secondary fermentation has settled into a steady blub-blub-blub of CO_2 through the water lock, go away and leave the cider alone until March (eight to twelve weeks). By this time, the fermentation should be completed, with clear cider on top of a thick yeast cake.

Bill prefers to rack his cider off the sediment and put it into another sanitized five-gallon carboy or stainless-steel keg before bottling off into sanitized twenty-two-ounce beer bottles. The still uncarbonated cider is allowed to age for a few months before being chilled and served.

TIM'S FIREHOUSE CIDER

In New England towns and villages, volunteer firefighters are as much a part of the social fabric as town meetings and church suppers. Tim Tierney is one of our unsung heroes, and he's a crackerjack cidermaker as well. His Firehouse Cider has a rich base of white and brown sugars that balance well against the spicy orange peel and cinnamon. The cider is turned by wild yeast, and the process is simple. After battling a hot blaze or rescuing a cold kitty from a tree, this is his favorite libation and one that deserves a try.

Ingredients for a stainless-steel pony keg (7 3/4 gallons):

> **7 1/2 gallons fresh pressed sweet cider**
> **4 cups dark brown sugar**
> **4 cups cane sugar**
> **1 jar (approximately 2 ounces) dried, grated orange peel**
> **2 tablespoons ground cinnamon**

Put the sugars, dried orange peel, and cinnamon in the keg. Pour in the sweet cider until the keg is filled to the bunghole and cover with plastic wrap to keep out vinegar flies. In a few days, when the cider starts working, remove the plastic wrap and let the cider do its thing. Wipe down the sides of the keg daily with sanitizing solution and paper towels. In a few weeks, as primary fermentation slows and the cider ceases foaming up and out of the keg, wipe the inside of the bunghole carefully and attach a fermentation lock.

Leave the cider alone until March or at least two months after CO_2 stops blub-blub-blubbing through the water lock. Rack the cider off the sediment into a clean sanitized container. Boil and cool three-fourths cup cane sugar and two cups water and add the resulting syrup to the cider. Siphon the cider into sanitized sixteen-ounce bottles and cap. Let the hard cider carbonate and mellow for at least two months before enjoying. As a tribute to those who risk their lives for us, raise your first glass of Firehouse Cider to firefighters everywhere.

BIT O' HONEY CYSER

Cidermakers often use honey to raise the specific gravity to the proper levels. However, if enough honey is used or honey is the sole adjunct to the point that a honeyed aroma and taste is noticeable, the beverage is known as cyser.

Cyser is a remarkable beverage because sweet apple cider and honey complement each other so well. The sweet cider contains all the enzymes and other nutrients needed for a healthy fermentation, while the honey contributes the necessary sugars and complex flavors.

Dark-colored or strong-tasting honeys will overpower the apple tastes if used in quantity, so include milder honeys such as store-purchased generic or clover. Apple cider is a perfect medium to show off the unique aromas and tastes of locally made honeys. Many cidermakers' reputations have been enhanced by cysers containing such honeys as orange blossom, cactus pear, apple, or cranberry. While in the orchards, watch out for hives between the rows of the various fruit trees or berry bushes, then inquire to see if some honey may be had.

This is a wonderful cyser with a delicate aroma and subtle taste. It is a bit lower in alcohol than other cysers and therefore most suitable for summertime picnics and outings.

Ingredients for five gallons:

> **5 gallons fresh pressed sweet cider, tested and adjusted for acid**
> **2 pounds clover honey (or enough to bring the specific gravity up to**

approximately 1.065)
ale or mead (honey wine) yeast
starter

Simmer the honey with a bit of cider over a low flame until the honey warms and thins. Pour a gallon of sweet cider into a sanitized glass carboy. Add the warmed honey then fill the carboy to its shoulders with sweet cider. Pitch the yeast, top off with the remaining sweet cider, and cover the top of the carboy with plastic wrap. You are using ale or mead yeast, so keep the cider between 65 and 75 degrees F (18 and 24 degrees C).

Fermentation begins very slowly as the heavier honey settles, then works very rapidly as the yeast feast on the large amounts of sugar in the blend. Wipe up and sanitize the overflow, and when it settles down, top off and add a fermentation lock.

The procedures for cyser are identical to cider with a notable exception: honey is a much more complex sugar than cane or corn sugars, meaning honey takes a long time to clear and an even longer time (at least six months) to ferment out and taste acceptable. Don't be over-anxious to bottle your cyser, let it ferment out completely (sometimes into midsummer) unless you want gushers or exploding bottles.

The taste of young cyser makes the most remarkable transformation as it ages. It is often bitter and even musty smelling and tasting during the first three or four months in the bottle before blossoming into an exotic beverage with a candied aroma and honeyed taste. Because of the amount of honey used and the unfermentable agents in it, the cyser will finish dry but have a lingering honey sweetness. The combination will please those in the know and convince any skeptics about the extraordinary quality and variety of beverages made from the noble apple.

Cyser may be bottled still and capped or corked, or may be made sparkling with the addition of a simple syrup of one-half cup sugar and two cups water (boiled for five minutes and cooled) to five gallons of cyser.

Let the bottled cyser age in a cool place for at least four months before drinking — you won't be disappointed!

GORMAN'S ROBUST CYSER

Every once in a while, a beverage is made that proves perfection exists. This is the case with Gorman's Robust Cyser. Tom Gorman is a superior homebrewer who becomes Star of the Day every time he shares his stash of Robust Cyser. This is not a gentle sipper, it's a head-spinning beverage of magnificent proportions. It is so rich in taste, so very smooth, so beautifully balanced that caution is thrown to the wind as I gratefully accept another glass (but not before turning the car keys over to a teetotaling friend).

Ingredients for five gallons:

> **5 gallons fresh pressed sweet cider**
> **(tested and adjusted for acid)**
> **7 pounds mild honey (or enough to**
> **bring the specific gravity up to**
> **approximately 1.150)**
> **1 tablespoon ground cinnamon**
> **1 pack dried Epernay wine yeast or**
> **yeast culture**

Warm the honey with a gallon of cider over a low flame to thin it before adding it and the cinnamon to the carboy full of sweet cider. Pitch the yeast or yeast culture and ferment as for Bit o' Honey Cyser recipe. Two things to note:

1. Epernay wine yeast is used because it has a high tolerance for alcohol. It will ferment more of the honey before settling out than will a low-tolerance beer yeast.

2. With such a large amount of honey, fermenting this cider and achieving the proper balance of tastes may take considerable time, maybe up to a year, so be patient. Take conso-

lation not only in the superior quality of this cyser but also in its longevity, for this cyser will keep in the bottle for up to four years.

APPLE BEER

This recipe requires the cidermaker to also be versed in brewing, because the beverage is more beer than cider (what a great excuse to learn how to brew). The ingredients seem to be quite different, but they all come together in a most satisfying beverage. The taste is rich with malt, cider, and honey but remains refreshing with the cinnamon and citrus overtones. Apple Beer takes a little more time to mellow than most beers.

Ingredients for five gallons:

> **6.6 pounds unhopped light malt extract (two cans)**
> **2 gallons sweet cider**
> **1 pound clover honey**
> **1 teaspoon Irish moss**
> **1 ounce Northern Brewer or 2 ounces Cascade leaf hops for bittering**
> **1 ounce Cascade leaf hops for aroma**
> **1 pack lager or ale yeast, liquid or dried**
> **1 tablespoon dried orange peel**
> **1 teaspoon ground cinnamon**

Bring three gallons of water to a boil in a five-gallon nonreactive pot (stainless steel or glass). At boil, add the malt extract and honey, stirring it to prevent scorching. Resume the boil and add half the bittering hops. Half an hour later, add the other half of the bittering hops and the Irish moss. After another thirty minutes, add the finishing hops and turn off the heat, letting the hops steep for five minutes (keep covered). Then, gently pour in the sweet cider before cooling the mixture (now called wort). To cool the wort, place the entire pot, with the lid still on, in a sink full of cold water. Keep refilling the sink, without

getting any water in the pot, until the pot is close to room temperature.

Strain the cooled wort into a sanitized five- or seven-gallon glass carboy and pitch the yeast. Stick one end of a one-inch diameter clear plastic tube into the mouth of your full carboy (should be a tight fit) and the other end into a bowl partially filled with a light sanitizing solution to create a safe air lock or blow-off tube. If using a seven gallon container, put the lid on tightly and seal with a bored-rubber stopper and a fermentation lock.

After primary fermentation, rack the Apple Beer into a sanitized five-gallon carboy and add the orange peel and cinnamon. Top off with either boiled and cooled cider or water and allow it to ferment to finish. Rack, prime, and bottle following regular procedure.

This beer benefits from an extended aging (for beer) of up to four months because it takes time for all the flavors to mesh. (Don't hesitate to call or stop by your local homebrew shop for some advice. Homebrewers are always glad to help a newcomer avoid some of the possible trouble spots of brewing.)

HOLIDAY SPICED CIDER

This is a festive and flavorful cider that once again demonstrates how versatile cider is. The aroma reminds some people of cold winters warmed by cups of hot mulled cider. For me, however, the memories are of a slice of warmed apple pie washed down with a glass of the hard stuff straight from the barrel. Start your own memories with a carboy of this spiced cider.

Ingredients for five gallons:

> **5 gallons fresh pressed sweet cider**
> **4 cups cane or corn sugar**
> **1 cup grade-A real maple syrup**
> **1 teaspoon ground cinnamon**
> **1 teaspoon ground cloves**
> **1 teaspoon allspice**

**1 teaspoon ground nutmeg
ale or lager beer yeast culture**

Make sure you use real maple syrup and not sugary pancake syrup. Beware of the lower grades of syrup because they are darker and have a more pronounced taste.

Put the sweet cider, sugar, and syrup into a sanitized carboy within two inches of the top, pitch the active yeast culture, and cover the opening with plastic wrap until the cider starts working. When fermentation starts, remove the wrap, and let the cider foam come up and out of the carboy. Follow good cleansing practices by wiping down the carboy daily with sanitizing solution.

Within two or three weeks the very active stages of primary fermentation will have subsided. Add the spices and top off with fresh cider before attaching a water lock. Let the cider continue to do its thing until early spring or until the cider is completely fermented and clear (usually eight to twelve weeks).

This cider is best with some festive sparkle, so siphon it into a clean container that already has a boiled and cooled solution of one-half cup sugar and one cup of water in it. Then bottle and cap it as you would any other cider.

This cider makes a great gift, so why not bottle it in large champagne bottles and decorate them with fancy ribbon? It will be the hit of the Thanksgiving or holiday meal.

GINGERED HONEY CIDER

Gingered Honey Cider is another spiced cider that is just too festive to enjoy without sharing. A small amount of honey gives this cider just a hint of sweetness, while the fresh ginger really perks up taste and aroma. I really like ginger, so the amount suggested is on the heavy side. If you prefer just a tease use the lesser amount.

Although an ale yeast may be used, a lager yeast and cold fermentation is prefer-

able for the clean, crisp taste it will contribute to the cider.

Ingredients for five gallons:

**5 gallons fresh pressed sweet cider
3 cups cane or corn sugar
2 cups clover or other mild honey
1 to 4 ounces freshly grated ginger
lager or ale beer yeast culture**

Dissolve the sugars and honey in one gallon of warmed cider and add to the other four gallons already in the sanitized carboy. Pitch the active yeast culture, fill the carboy to within two inches of the top and cover the opening with plastic wrap. Keep the carboy at room temperature until fermentation starts, then carefully move the carboy to a cool place, below 55 degrees F (13 degrees C).

Primary fermentation at these temperatures will last at least one month, so remember to wipe down the carboy daily with sanitizing solution. At the end of primary fermentation, add the freshly grated ginger, top off the carboy with fresh cider, and attach a fermentation lock.

At this point, the cider may be left to ferment at cool temperatures. Secondary fermentation is characterized by a steady stream of rising bubbles that slowly subside then cease when all the sugars have been converted. By the end of this two- to three-month fermentation period, the cider is clear and ready to bottle.

Even though the fermentation process will have been completed, it may take a few months for the flavors of Gingered Honey Cider to mellow. At bottling, the ginger will still be sharp and not yet blended into the apple and honey base. But don't worry, this is one fabulous-tasting cider. All it needs is time.

I prefer this as a sparkling cider, although it may be bottled still. Again, rack the cider into a sanitized five-gallon container and add a boiled and cooled solution of one-half cup sugar and one cup water before bottling and capping. The aging process will take place after the cider is bottled, so let it sit quietly for a few months before drinking.

When the proper time comes, go down to the cellar with an opener and a clean, clear piece of glassware. Open the bottle and slowly pour. The tiny bubbles enhance the golden color and liberate the ginger aromas as the first draught is taken. The honeyed apple flavors flow past the lips and over the tongue before the warming aftertaste of ginger reminds the imbiber that yes indeed, patience is a virtue and, yes indeed, you are a cidermaster.

Judging & Evaluating Cider

It is important to evaluate your own cider and to have others, experienced or not, give their impressions of your house beverage. You'll acquire knowledge from the pros because of their hands-on experience. You'll get the straight scoop from cider rookies because they may evaluate your hard cider simply by whether it tastes good or bad.

On-the-spot, unrehearsed evaluations of cider are a part of the life of the cidermaker. Surroundings such as a cool cellar, a spring cider bottling party, or a glorious autumn afternoon in the back yard enhance cider's appeal and make for good times with family and friends. However, to critically evaluate and judge hard cider in a fair manner takes more than a few words of praise or criticism. A fair tasting requires a level playing field, a working vocabulary to describe what you are tasting, and a certain knowledge of ciders, wines, or beers.

Cider tastings and judgings can be as serious as the American Homebrewers Association® National Homebrew Competition, which judges home-made ciders from around the country in four different cider categories, or as casual as a cookout in the back yard. Regardless of the atmosphere, certain items are essential to an enjoyable and educational cider event.

SETTING UP A TASTING

Putting together a cider tasting or competition does not take a huge amount of intense planning or a large sum of money. After notifying a group of cidermakers of your plans, gathering a few simple items and a few helpers is the largest obstacle you'll face. Remember to have enough supplies for every cider and every judge; uniformity is important to ensure that just the ciders are being compared, and not the glasses, or any other outside factors.

• Tables and chairs may seem obvious, but filling out score sheets on your lap while being swallowed up in an overstuffed easy chair is no easy task. Straightback chairs at the dining room table are fine. If outdoors, sturdy folding tables and chairs or even a picnic table will do. A few extra tables won't hurt because everybody should have plenty of room to spread out glasses and papers. Above all, it must be comfortable to sit and write. A white tablecloth or table covering is also important as a background to clearly see the true colors of the cider.

• Glasses and spittoons are essential because a lot of liquid is sloshing about at a tasting and you should be adequately prepared to dispense and dispose of it. First, consider that in a normal flight of ciders (the number of ciders tasted at one time) up to a dozen samples will be tasted by each judge. Unless the host has plenty of glasses, common sense dictates the use of inexpensive clear plastic glasses of at least an eight-ounce capacity. These are commonly used for sanctioned beer and cider competitions. Glasses often carry soap or detergent residues that can damage the flavor and aroma of a cider, so plastic is usually the best way to go.

Spittoons are a necessary precaution to protect the tongues of your tasters or judges. Most cider is tasted and spit out to prevent palate fatigue (or gustatory shell shock). Most of the water poured to rinse one's mouth is spit out as well. You don't have to provide every judge with an old copper tobacco spittoon, a simple one-half- or one-gallon plastic bucket will suffice. These are used by the food-service industry for potato salad, scallops, tapioca pudding, etc. Ask the deli manager at your local supermarket for several such containers. You may have to pay 50 cents or so for each or you may be able to work out a trade for a bottle or two of cider. (Several clean trash cans are also important, as these events tend to generate quite a bit of debris.)

• Palate cleansers, such as plain, unsalted bread, breadsticks, or crackers, are effective mouth sponges. A gallon jug or two of cool water is also a good idea. Avoid flavored seltzers or high-mineral content spring waters.

• A few different scoring sheets are used by agricultural organizations and amateur beer/cider clubs. Sheets used for American Homebrewers Association sanctioned and/or national competitions are preferred because of the helpful descriptive definitions printed on the sheet itself as well as the clear scoring outlines. However, it doesn't really matter which one you use as long as you have plenty of them. Clipboards that hold them together are useful, as well as a large supply of sharpened pencils.

Cider should be sampled blind for a formal tasting, meaning that the origin and producer of each entry will be unknown to the panel of judges. Thus, every bottle should be free of any labels or markings except simple numerical or alphabetical designations assigned by the competition organizer.

Prior to the tasting, the ciders should be grouped by style (see subcategories of cider on p. 59) so that similar ciders are compared to one another as well as being judged individually. For each category a master list of entrants can be compiled and a number or letter assigned to each, which in turn can be written on a gummed label and affixed to the bottle. This code easily prevents mix-ups. A day or two prior to the tasting, box up the cider entries by category and chill them at 45 to 50 degrees F (7 to 13 degrees C). The day of the tasting, assign the judges to their respective boxes and let the judging commence.

THE COMPONENTS OF CIDER

Judging cider competently is a learned process, a combination of science and art, that requires a skilled palate to separate the components of tastes and smells into a structured analysis. These components must then be described using a certain vocabulary that is neither vague nor so flowery as to appear ridiculous. A common vocabulary also makes it easier for judges to understand each other's comments. In addition, each of the elements of cider (appearance, aroma, and flavor) is judged against accepted standards within each category and graded using a point system. Finally, each cider entry is compared to the other entries to determine their relative standings within each category. Make no mistake, to judge competently is not always a walk in the park (or a stroll in the orchard). However, with practice and persistence, judging cider can be an extremely rewarding and satisfying avocation.

The visual characteristic of cider are evident once it is poured into a glass. Even for the novice, aspects such as color and clarity are easily distinguished. Depending on the style or ingredients, cider color can range from a very pale straw yellow to yellow gold, or from a true gold to an amber or brown gold. The darker colors may indicate the use of honey, brown sugar, or molasses as adjuncts, whereas an orange-brown color may indicate that the cider has become oxidized and is past drinking. The presence of green or orange hues in an otherwise light-colored cider, may indicate problems.

If the cider is sparkling, observe the bubbles. A naturally sparkling cider (one primed with sugar and carbonated by yeast) will have tiny beading bubbles that swirl up to the top. A force-carbonated cider (one carbonated with CO_2) will have large bubbles that rise straight to the top.

Note the degree of clarity. The cider should be clear or, even better, brilliant. Because most ciders are made without additives or preservatives and are not filtered, a very slight haze may be apparent and should not detract too much from its overall clarity. Remember to be careful not to disturb the sediment at the bottom of bottles of naturally carbonated cider. Pour the cider out slowly and don't tip the bottle all the way up, leaving the yeast and a few drops of cider in the bottle.

Bouquet/aroma should be obvious when you put your nose into the glass and take a few short, strong sniffs ... don't be shy. The smell should have a noticeable apple fragrance along with aromas from any added fruits or spices. Lighter styles of cider should have more lively aromas with fragrant overtones of the more common apple varieties (such as Delicious or McIntosh) than the more robust styles of cider.

Heavier styles with varied adjuncts and higher attenuating yeast should reflect this in the bouquet. The addition of honey for a cyser will give the cider a meadlike sweet aroma. The fact that many cidermakers use more durable wine or champagne yeasts for their higher alcohol ciders will be reflected in a winelike or yeastlike aroma. Also note that wild yeast-turned ciders should have very complex and exotic aromas.

Regardless of the style or type of cider, the aroma should never be stinky or smelly (which definitely means big problems) and beware of a very sharp, although still appley, aroma. Such aromas are called acetic and may mean the cider in the glass is closer to salad dressing than drinking cider because it has turned to vinegar.

Flavor is the primary factor to consider when evaluating a cider. To get the full flavor try "chewing" the cider. This incorporates air, which helps the cider breathe and release its full flavor. The goal of tasting the cider is twofold: (1) to confirm or refute what has already been noted about the appearance and bouquet of the cider and (2) to break down the taste into the following characteristics:

• Acidity (from the malic acid in apples) is the backbone on which all other flavor elements of a good cider are supported. Acidity gives cider zest and liveliness and assures that the cider is healthy. Too much acidity, enough to make one's mouth pucker, is obviously a fault.

• Dryness or sweetness is easily identifiable by the absence or presence of residual sugars on your tongue. Cider may be dry (different than tart), off-dry, semi-dry, semi-sweet, or sweet depending on the style of the cider. The sweeter the cider, the more it must be balanced by acidity to prevent it from being candy or syrupy sweet.

• Body is the guts of the cider. Alcohol content and richness of taste will determine if a cider is light or full bodied. Note that cider with a light body is not considered a bad cider, but cider referred to as thin lacks taste and body and needs some fine tuning on the next batch.

APPLES SORTED BY VARIETY AT THE GREENWOOD FARM

PHOTO BY: CHARLIE OLCHOWSKI

• Balance is the key indiction of a superior cider. Cidermakers strive for balance of all the components of their ciders. For example, a dessert-style cider is balanced by plenty of acidity, and a robust high-alcohol cider is balanced by tannin. One flavor does not dominate the entire mouthful, rather, a series of flavors and sensations flows over the tongue culminating in a lip smacking aaaaahhhh.

• Aftertaste or finish is the last hurrah from a mouthful of swallowed cider. Ideally, it is a crisp lingering taste that invites the next mouthful. Ciders lacking this are said to finish short.

• Drinkability and overall impression are catch-all sections where the judge can commend the cidermaker on a job well done ("I liked this! Send me more!"), relay tips on how improve certain aspects of the cider, or clarify points made on the judging sheet. On some scoring sheets, this section is worth points and the judge can then fine tune scoring between ciders of similar quality.

In conclusion, be aware that taste is also very subjective and personal. The goal of a judging is more than evaluating and categorizing. Praise the cidermakers who have turned out superior bottles, be understanding and constructive with criticism to those who have fermented a cider less (or very less) than perfect. Above all, be honest about your

impressions and remember to enjoy yourself because you are a participant in the revival of this country's great natural beverage.

There are four categories under which cider can be entered for an American Homebrewers Association sanctioned competition. Note that if a small number of entries are found in a particular category, that category may be "collapsed" (incorporated) into another to facilitate the judging.

1. Still: Not effervescent. Under 7 percent alcohol by volume (5.5 percent by weight). Can be dry or sweet. Pale yellow color, must be clear or brilliant. Apple aroma. Light body and crisp apple flavor. Sugar adjuncts may be used.

2. Sparkling: Effervescent but not foamy. May be force carbonated. No head. Under 8 percent alcohol by volume (6.3 percent by weight). Dry or sweet. Pale yellow color, must be clear or brilliant. Light to medium body, crisp apple taste. Sugar adjuncts may be used.

3. New England Style: Still or sparkling dry cider. Carbonation must be natural. Between 8 and 14 percent alcohol by volume (6.3 and 11 percent by weight). Pale to medium-yellow color. Pronounced apple aroma. Medium to full body. Balanced by drying tannins but never "hot" due to excess

alcohol. Adjuncts include white and brown sugars, molasses, or raisins. Wild or wine yeast only.

4. Specialty Cider: Any and all adjuncts may be used. Alcohol content must be below 14 percent by volume (11 percent by weight). Total unfermented juice must be composed of at least 75 percent apple juice.

With these style guidelines, the recipes from chapter ten, and the following cider score sheets from the American Homebewer Association, you'll be making competition-winning cider in no time. But don't stop there. Continue to develop your own cider-making techniques and styles. Create your own recipes. Talk with other cidermakers to learn their secrets and to teach them yours. After all, cidermaking is an art, and you are now one of the masters.

American Homebrewers Association
1994 National Homebrew Competition

CIDER SCORE SHEET

The following is the 1994 American Homebrewers Association's cider score sheet. The score sheet is updated annually and used in homebrew competitions. For more information on the National Homebrew Competition or Sanctioned Competition Program, call or write the American Homebrewers Association, PO Box 1679, Boulder, CO 80306-1679, U.S.A.; (303) 447-0816, FAX (303) 447-2825.

DESCRIPTOR DEFINITIONS

✔ CHECK WHENEVER APPROPRIATE

☐ **Acetic**—A vinegarlike smell and sharp taste, a distinct fault.

☐ **Acidity**—Malic acid is responsible for the freshness, zing in cider.

☐ **Alcoholic**—The general effect of ethanol and higher alcohols. Tastes warming.

☐ **Astringent**—A drying sensation in the mouth similar to chewing on a teabag. Due to excess tannin and acceptable only in a young cider.

☐ **Aftertaste**—The lingering taste in the back of the throat. Ideally long and pleasant.

☐ **Balanced**—No component of the cider overpowers another. An alcoholic cider is balanced by tannin, a sweet cider is balanced by crisp acidity.

☐ **Body**—The "middle" of a mouthful of cider. Good body will feel heavy in the mouth.

☐ **Bouquet**—Also known as the smell, nose, or aroma.

☐ **Carbonation**—A naturally carbonated cider has small beading bubbles. An artificially carbonated cider has large, uniform bubbles.

☐ **Clarity**—The visual aspect of cider. It may be brilliant, clear, slight haze, haze, or cloudy.

☐ **Clean**—Free of apparent off odors or tastes.

☐ **Color**—Pale yellow, light yellow, yellow, golden. Green tinge or orange hues signify potential problems.

☐ **Dry**—A sensation on the tongue that indicates lack of residual sugar. Varies from bone dry to dry, off-dry and semi-dry.

☐ **Fruity**—May be fruity in flavor and not unpleasant, or fruity in bouquet and not unpleasant either. Quite common due to the aromatic quality of the popular McIntosh apple.

☐ **Hot**—A fault due to excess alcohol.

☐ **Light**—Refers to body and is not a negative, as opposed to thin.

☐ **Metallic**—Caused by exposure to metal. Also described as tinny, coins, bloodlike. Check your brewpot and caps.

☐ **Moldy (musty)**—A closed in, sherrylike smell, like damp cardboard. Due to oxidation or rarely to overzealous filtration.

☐ **Mousy**—A disorder due to lactic-acid bacteria. Cider smells and tastes like a rodent's den.

☐ **New England-style Cider**—A strong cider (+8% alc.) made following traditional methods.

☐ **Phenolic**—A plasticlike taste/smell caused by some wild yeasts or bacteria.

☐ **Sparkling**—Having carbonation.

☐ **Still**—Lacking carbonation.

☐ **Sulfury**—Smells like burnt matches. Due to high temperature fermentation or excess use of SO_2.

☐ **Sweet**—Basic taste associated with sugar. May be appropriate for style as in a dessert cider.

☐ **Thin**—Lacking body or "stuffing."

☐ **Woody**—A taste or aroma due to an extended length of time in oak or on wood chips.

☐ **Yeasty**—A breadlike aroma due to a cider sitting on its lees for an extended period.

☐ **Young**—A cider with components that have not yet matured into a balanced whole.

American Homebrewers Association
1994 National Homebrew Competition

Round No. _____ **Entry No.** _____

Category No._____

Subcategory (spell out) _____

Judged By (please print)_____

Judge Qualifications (check one) ☐ Recognized ☐ Certified

☐ National ☐ Master ☐ Experienced (but not in BJCP)

☐ Apprentice or Novice ☐ Other: _____

BOTTLE INSPECTION Comments_____

_____

	Max. Score
BOUQUET/AROMA (as appropriate for style)	10 _____

Expression of ingredients as appropriate

Comments _____

_____

_____

_____

APPEARANCE (as appropriate for style)   6_____

Color (3), Clarity (3)

Comments _____

_____

_____

FLAVOR (as appropriate for style) _____   24 _____

Balance of adicity, sweetness, alcohol strength, and body carbonation (if appropriate) (14).
Other ingredients as appropriate (5), Aftertaste (5)

Comments _____

_____

_____

DRINKABILITY & OVERALL IMPRESSION   10 _____

Comments _____

_____

_____

TOTAL (50 possible points):_____

Scoring Guide		
Excellent (40-50):	Exceptionally exemplifies style, requires little or no attention	
Very Good (30-39):	Exemplifies style well, requires some attention	
Good (25-29):	Exemplifies style satisfactorily, but requires attention	
Drinkable (20-24):	Does not exemplify style, requires attention	
Problem (<20):	Problematic, requires much attention	
	Use other side for additional comments.	NHC94

Glossary

Acetobacter
A harmful bacteria that produces vinegarlike smells and tastes caused by of the presence of oxygen or high temperatures.

Acidity
Several types of acids are responsible for the refreshing zing in cider, most notably malic and lactic acids.

Adjunct
Any ingredient, sugar, or spice that is added and fermented with the sweet cider.

Airlock
(see fermentation lock)

Airspace
(see ullage)

Alcohol by volume (v/v)
The percentage of volume of alcohol per volume of cider. To calculate the approximate volumetric alcohol content, subtract the terminal gravity from the original gravity and divide the result by .0075. For example: 1.050-1.012 = .038 / .0075 = 5% v/v.

Alcohol by weight (w/v)
The percentage weight of alcohol per volume of cider. For example: 3.2 percent alcohol by weight = 3.2 grams of alcohol per 100 centiliters of cider.

Aldehyde
A contraction of alcohol dehydrogenate. These compounds are characterized as oxidized alcohols, with a terminal CHO group.

Ale
A type of beer fermented by warm-temperature, top-fermenting yeast known as Saccharomyces cerevisiae. Ale yeast contribute fruity tastes and aromas when used to ferment cider.

Amino acids
The building blocks of proteins. Essential components of must (unfermented grape or apple juice), required for adaquate yeast growth.

Aroma
The smell of the cider should be of apples and whatever adjuncts were used.

Attenuation

The reduction in the must's specific gravity caused by the transformation of sugars into alcohol and carbon-dioxide gas.

Bacteria

Single-celled micro-organisms that are the notorious "uninvited guests" of the fermentation cycle because they generally putrefy cider with disastrous results. Practice good sanitary procedures and keep the air out.

Balanced

None of the components of the cider overpowers any other. Acid balances sweet, alcohol balances tannin.

Balling

A saccharometer invented by Carl Joseph Napoleon Balling in 1843. It is calibrated for 63.5 degrees F (17.5 degrees C), and graduated in grams per hundred, giving a direct reading of the percentage of extract by weight per 100 grams solution. For example: 10 °B = 10 grams of sugar per 100 grams of must.

Blow-by (blow-off)

A single-stage cidermaking fermentation method in which a plastic tube is fitted into the mouth of a carboy, with the other end submerged in a pail of sterile water. Unwanted residues and carbon dioxide are expelled through the tube, while air is prevented from coming into contact with the fermenting cider, thus avoiding contamination.

Body

The "weight" of the cider in the mouth. A rich cider will be heavy, a lighter style will be light.

Campden tablets

Premeasured sodium metabisulfite pills used to rid cider of almost all organisms prior to fermentation or bottling.

Carbon dioxide

The fizz in the flask. Naturally carbonated cider has small beading bubbles. Force-carbonated cider has larger, more sodalike bubbles.

Carbonation

The process of introducing carbon-dioxide gas into a liquid by: 1. injecting the finished cider with carbon dioxide; 2. adding young fermenting cider to finished cider for a renewed fermentation (kraeusening); 3. priming (adding sugar) to fermented cider prior to bottling, creating a secondary fermentation in the bottle.

Carboy

Big five-, six and a half-, or seven-gallon glass jugs used to ferment cider. Their advantages are numerous: you can see the cider inside, they're easy to clean, relatively inexpensive, and corks and waterlocks fit easily into their narrow neck. The one disadvantage is obvious, breakability. Try placing them inside plastic milk crates for extra protection.

Chill haze

Haziness caused by protein and tannin during the secondary fermentation.

Clean

A cider that is free of odors and tastes.

Cyser

A cider whose main adjunct is honey as opposed to a honeyed cider, which contains a lesser amount of honey.

Dimethyl sulfide (DMS)
An important sulfur-carrying compound originating in malt. Adds crisp, "lager-like" character at low levels and corn or cabbage flavors at high levels.

Dry
A cider with no apparent residual sweetness. Also, a fully fermented cider is said to be "fermented to dry."

Ester
A class of organic compounds created from the reaction of an alcohol and an organic acid. These tend to have fruity aromas and are detectable at low concentrations.

Fermentation
The process by which yeast convert sugars to carbon dioxide (CO_2) and alcohol.

Fermentation lock
A one-way valve, which allows carbon-dioxide gas to escape from the fermenter while excluding contaminants.

Final specific gravity
The specific gravity of a cider when fermentation is complete.

Fining
A procedure used more frequently by brewers and winemakers than cidermakers to clear their beers and wines (pectic enzyme already in apples does this naturally). A clarifying agent, such as gelatin or beaten egg whites, is added to the alcoholic liquid to "catch" small particles. The mass then falls to the bottom of the fermenter, and the clear liquid is racked off the top.

Flocculation
The behavior of yeast cells joining into masses and settling out toward the end of fermentation.

Hard cider
Fresh sweet cider that has been fermented, as opposed to a "soft" drink such as cola. This is not indicative of quality. The term hard cider is only used in the United States. In the United Kingdom, it is redundant because cider is already alcoholic having once been apple juice.

Honeyed
Characteristic aromas of cyser, especially of an older, mature bottle of robust cider that used darker sugars as adjuncts.

Hydrometer
A glass instrument used to measure the specific gravity of liquids as compared to water, consisting of a graduated stem resting on a weighed float.

Isinglass
A gelatinous substance made from the swim bladder of certain fish and added to cider as a fining agent.

Lactic acid
$C_3H_6O_3$ aerobic (requiring oxygen) lactic bacteria that converts malic acid into lactic acid and CO_2 after primary fermentation. This malo-lactic fermentation is desirable because it subdues the sharp malic acid and makes the cider smoother in taste. Both the lactic bacteria and the malic acid occur naturally in the juice. This is a rare case of desirable bacteria! Beware that lactic bacteria may turn nasty if cider is stored too warm, above 70 degrees F (21 degrees C) or if the juice is low in acid (too many Red Delicious apples in the blend), in which case sour tastes and horrid aromas may develop. Therefore, remember to test and adjust the acids and keep the cider cool.

Lager

A type of beer fermented by cool-temperature, bottom-fermenting yeast known as Saccharomyces uvarum. When used to ferment cider, lager yeast contribute clean dry tastes and aromas.

Lees

The sediment made up of spent yeast cells, bits of apple, and other solids that settle on the bottom of the fermenter.

Malic acid

$C_4H_6O_5$ is a crystalline acid found in many fruits, especially apples. It is characterized by a zesty, Granny Smith-like apple taste and is desirable to balance the syrupy sugars.

Mead

A very old beverage originating in England made from boiling together honey and water, then cooling and fermenting.

Must

Unfermented grape or apple juice.

New England-style cider

A strong cider that uses a variety of sugars, spices, and raisins. This cider was made in wooden barrels for ages but may be made using modern equipment (glass carboys, stainless-steel kegs) with traditional ingredients, especially wild yeasts.

Original gravity

The specific gravity of must previous to fermentation. A measure of the total amount of dissolved solids in must.

Petillant

A French term used to describe wines that are neither flat nor sparkling. Bubbles are not pronounced, but, when tasted, a refreshing tingle is apparent on the tongue. Newly bottled ciders or those that are freshly kegged are usually petillant.

pH

A measure of acidity or alkalinity of a solution, usually on a scale of one to fourteen, where seven is neutral.

Pitch

This refers simply to the act of adding the dried yeast or active yeast culture to the sweet cider to start fermentation.

Plato

A saccharometer that expresses specific gravity as extract weight in a one-hundred-gram solution at 68 degrees F (20 degrees C). A revised, more accurate version of Balling, developed by Dr. Plato.

Polyphenol

Complexes of phenolic compounds involved in chill haze formation and oxidative staling.

Primary fermentation

The first of the two stages of fermentation characterized by much visible activity in the fermenter because the yeast feast on the sugars and burp out alcohol and CO_2. Foam and bits of apple push up and out of the open carboy as zillions of tiny bubbles rise rapidly through the cider. After a month, the young cider may be racked off the lees from the primary fermentor (where primary stage happened) to the secondary fermenter (where the second stage will occur).

Priming

Adding a sugar solution to a still cider before bottling so that fermentation occurs in the bottle, carbonating the cider. This process turns still cider into sparkling cider.

Priming sugar

A small amount of corn, malt, or cane sugar added to bulk cider, prior to racking or at bottling, to induce a new fermentation and create carbonation.

Racking

The process of transferring cider from one container to another, especially into the final package (bottles, kegs, etc.).

Saccharometer

An instrument that determines the sugar concentration of a solution by measuring the specific gravity.

Sanitize

The simple yet necessary process to ensure your cider does not become contaminated by uninvited guests. Once your equipment is clean (free of visible dirt and grime), sanitize everything by soaking or rinsing your stuff in a solution of bleach, B-Brite, or any other approved chemical to rid it of any undesirable bacteria or wild yeast.

Secondary fermentation

The second, less-active stage of fermentation is characterized by a mellowing of tastes and gradual clearing. After the cider is racked into the secondary fermenter, a waterlock is attached to keep out the air. Subtle changes occur as the tastes mellow and blend. As the yeast go dormant and fall to the bottom of the fermenter, the cider clears, gradually at first, before becoming brilliant. This period lasts up to three months until bottling time.

Sparkling

Cider that is bubbly. Cider may be made to sparkle naturally by bottle fermentation, i.e. adding a measured amount of sugar to the cider before capping (thank you Dom Perignon!), or the cider may be force carbonated at the last minute by attaching a CO_2 container to a keg of still cider.

Specific gravity

The density of a liquid compared to that of pure water which is given the value of 1.000 at 39.2 degrees F (4 degrees C). Sweet cider contains sugars that make the liquid more dense, thus a higher reading (around 1.050). As sweet cider ferments, the amount of sugar is reduced as lighter gravity alcohol is produced. This gives steadily lower readings as the cider becomes more alcoholic and less sweet.

Starter

A batch of fermenting yeast, added to the must to initiate fermentation.

Still

A beverage that lacks carbonation. This is not the same as flat, which indicates a beverage that has lost its fizz.

Sugar solution

A premeasured dosage of boiled and cooled sugar and water added to dry cider just before bottling to produce a bottle fermentation, thus sparkling cider. The standard amount for a five-gallon batch is one-half cup of sugar to one cup of water.

Tannin

(See polyphenol)

Ullage

The empty space between a liquid and the top of its container. Also called airspace or headspace.

v/v

(see alcohol by volume)

w/v

(see alcohol by weight)

Water hardness

The amount of dissolved minerals in water.

Wild yeast

Uncultured yeast strains. They may be beneficial and capable of turning sweet cider into a hard cider much more complex than the best cultured variety, or they may turn cider into something awful. They tend to be indigenous to certain orchards and only experience will indicate if the specific yeasts on the apples will make great cider. By the same token, wild yeasts indigenous to specific vineyards make some of the world's finest wines (Chateau Latour and Ridge Vineyards).

Yeast

Micro-organisms that promote fermentation by consuming sugars and expelling alcohol and carbon dioxide. Yeasts are responsible for the fermentation of beer, cider, and wine as well as the raising of bread. Without these guys, the world would be, by many accounts, much duller.

Bibliography

Books:

-*All About Apples*. Martin, Alice A. Houghton Mifflin Co., 1976.

-*American Cider Book,. The*. Orton, Vrest. Farrar, Straus and Giroux, 1973.

-*American Fruit Book The*. Cole, S.W. John P. Jewett Publisher, 1849.

- *Apple Book, The*. Sanders, Rosanne. Phaidon Press Ltd., 1988.

-*Apples*. Wynne, Peter. Hawthorne Books, 1975.

-*Apples, Apples, Apples*. Helfman, Elizabeth. T. Nelson, 1977.

- *Art of Making Wine, The*. Adkins, J. Walker Publishing Co., 1971.

-*Book of Country Things, A*. Needham, Walter. Stephen Green Press., 1965.

-*Christmas Customs and Traditions*. Muir, Frank. Taplinger Press, 1975.

-"Doomsday for cider ... or is there light at the end of the tunnel." Kitton, David. *What's Brewing*, October, 1992. CAMRA.

-*Early American Beverages*. Brown, John Hull. Crown Publishers, 1966.

-*History of Wilton, New Hampshire, 1762 - 1888*. Livermoore, Abiel. 1888.

-*Making Mead (Honey Wine): History, Recipes, Methods & Equipment*. Morse, R. Wicwas Press, 1980.

-*New Complete Joy of Home brewing, The*. Papazian, Charlie. Avon Press, 1991.

-*Paleolithic Cave Art*. Ucko, Peter J. and Rosenfield, Andree. Macgraw-Hill, 1967.

-*Practical Brewer, The*. Master Brewers Association of the Americas, 1977.

-*Smithsonian Timelines of the Ancient World: A Visual Chronology from the Origins of Life to A.D. 1500*. Scarre, Chris. Dorling Kindersley Inc., 1993.

-*Sweet and Hard Cider*. Proulx, Annie, and Nichols, Lew. Garden Way Publishing, 1980.

-*Technology of Wine Making, The*. AVI Publishing, 1980.

-*What's Brewing*. October 1993. CAMRA.

-*Wine Tasting and Wine Cellars*. Broadbent, M. Simon and Schuster, 1984.

Texts:

-*Apple Juice Workshop*. 1984.

-*Processed Apple Products Workshop*. 1985.

-*Processed Apples Research Report*. 1983.

-*Apple Seminar*. 1977.

The above texts were edited by Donald Downing at the Institute of Food Science at Cornell University.

- *"Pressing Cider in New England: Two Centuries of Technology Development."* Schumacher Jr., Gus.
- *"Hard Times for Cider."* Nicholson, J. Boston Phoenix, 1989.

Index

HOMEBREWER?

Join the thousands of American Homebrewers Association® members who read **Zymurgy** ® — the magazine for homebrewers and beer lovers.

Every issue of **Zymurgy** is full of tips, techniques, new recipes, new products, equipment and ingredient reviews, beer news, technical articles — the whole world of homebrewing. PLUS, the AHA brings members the National Homebrewers Conference, the National Homebrew Competition, the Beer Judge Certification Program, the Homebrew Club Network, periodic discounts on books from Brewers Publications and much, much more.

Photocopy and mail this coupon today to join the AHA or call now for credit card orders, (303) 546-6514.

Name

Address

City   State/Province

Zip/Postal Code   Country

Phone

☐ Enclosed is $29 for one full year.
Canadian memberships are $34 U.S., International memberships are $44 U.S.

☐ Please charge my credit card ☐ Visa ☐ MC

Card No.   —   —   —   Exp. Date

Signature

Make check to: American Homebrewers Association, PO Box 1510, Boulder, CO 80306, USA.
Offer valid until 3/1/96.   Prices subject to change.   CID95

BOOKS for Brewers and Beer Lovers

Order Now ... Your Brew Will Thank You!

These books offered by Brewers Publications are some of the most sought after reference tools for homebrewers and professional brewers alike. Filled with tips, techniques, recipes and history, these books will help you expand your brewing horizons. Let the world's foremost brewers help you as you brew. Whatever your brewing level or interest, Brewers Publications has the information necessary for you to brew the best beer in the world — your beer.

- -

Please send me more free information on the following: (check all that apply)

◊ Merchandise and Book Catalog
◊ American Homebrewers Association®
◊ Institute for Brewing Studies
◊ Great American Beer Festival®

Ship to:

Name

Address

City   State/Province

Zip/Postal Code   Country

Daytime Phone   (   )

Please use the following in conjunction with an order form when ordering books from Brewers Publications.

Payment Method

◊ Check or Money Order Enclosed (Payable to the Association of Brewers)
◊ Visa   ◊ MasterCard

Card Number   –   –   –   Expiration Date

Name on Card   Signature

Brewers Publications Inc., PO Box 1510, Boulder, CO 80306-1510, USA; (303) 546-6514, FAX (303) 447-2825.

CID 95

BREWERS PUBLICATIONS ORDER FORM

PROFESSIONAL BREWING BOOKS

QTY.	TITLE	STOCK #	PRICE	EXT. PRICE
_____	Brewery Planner	500	80.00	_____
_____	North American Brewers Resource Directory	505	80.00	_____
_____	Principles of Brewing Science	463	29.95	_____

THE BREWERY OPERATIONS SERIES
from Micro and Pubbrewers Conferences

QTY.	TITLE	STOCK #	PRICE	EXT. PRICE
_____	Volume 6, 1989 Conference	536	25.95	_____
_____	Volume 7, 1990 Conference	537	25.95	_____
_____	Volume 8, 1991 Conference, Brewing Under Adversity	538	25.95	_____
_____	Volume 9, 1992 Conference, Quality Brewing — Share the Experience	539	25.95	_____

CLASSIC BEER STYLE SERIES

QTY.	TITLE	STOCK #	PRICE	EXT. PRICE
_____	Pale Ale	401	11.95	_____
_____	Continental Pilsener	402	11.95	_____
_____	Lambic	403	11.95	_____
_____	Vienna, Märzen, Oktoberfest	404	11.95	_____
_____	Porter	405	11.95	_____
_____	Belgian Ale	406	11.95	_____
_____	German Wheat Beer	407	11.95	_____
_____	Scotch Ale	408	11.95	_____
_____	Bock	409	11.95	_____

BEER AND BREWING SERIES, for homebrewers and beer enthusiasts, from National Homebrewers Conferences

QTY.	TITLE	STOCK #	PRICE	EXT. PRICE
_____	Volume 8, 1988 Conference	448	21.95	_____
_____	Volume 10, 1990 Conference	450	21.95	_____
_____	Volume 11, 1991 Conference, Brew Free or Die!	451	21.95	_____
_____	Volume 12, 1992 Conference, Just Brew It!	452	21.95	_____

GENERAL BEER AND BREWING INFORMATION

QTY.	TITLE	STOCK #	PRICE	EXT. PRICE
_____	The Art of Cidermaking	468	9.95	_____
_____	Brewing Lager Beer	460	14.95	_____
_____	Brewing Mead	461	11.95	_____
_____	Dictionary of Beer and Brewing	462	19.95	_____
_____	Evaluating Beer	465	19.95	_____
_____	Great American Beer Cookbook	466	24.95	_____
_____	Victory Beer Recipes	467	11.95	_____
_____	Winners Circle	464	11.95	_____

SUBTOTAL _____

Call or write for a free *Beer Enthusiast* catalog today.

Colo. Residents Add 3% Sales Tax _____

• U.S. funds only.
• All Brewers Publications books come with a money-back guarantee.

P & H * _____

*Postage & Handling:** $4 for the first book ordered, plus $1 for each book thereafter. Canadian and international orders please add $5 for the first book and $2 for each book thereafter. Orders cannot be shipped without appropriate P&H.

TOTAL _____

Brewers Publications Inc., PO Box 1510, Boulder, CO 80306-1510, USA; (303) 546-6514, FAX (303) 447-2825.

Examine the World of

Microbrewing

and

Pubbrewing

Travel the world of commercial, small-scale brewing; the realm of microbrewers and pubbrewers.

The New Brewer magazine guides you through this new industry. Its pages introduce you to marketing, finance, operations, equipment, recipes, interviews — in short, the whole landscape.

Subscribe to *The New Brewer* and become a seasoned traveler.

No Risk Offer

Subscribe now and receive six issues. Money-back guarantee

$55 a year (U.S.) $65 (International) U.S. funds only

Published by the Institute for Brewing Studies, PO Box 1510, Boulder, CO 80306-1510, USA; (303) 546-6514.

The **New Brewer**

THE MAGAZINE FOR MICRO- AND PUB-BREWERS

The Award-winning

GREAT AMERICAN BEER COOKBOOK

From Brewers Publications and *zymurgy*'s® Brewgal Gourmet comes a cookbook like no other! All recipes use beer to enhance flavor potential, giving food an added culinary dimension — 217 recipes in all. Foreword by Michael Jackson.

Thanks to Brewers Publications and Candy Schermerhorn you can unlock the secrets to cooking with beer.

To receive your copy for only $24.95 (plus $4 P&H), call or write Brewers Publications at PO Box 1510, Boulder, CO 80306-1510, USA; (303) 546-6514, FAX (303) 447-2825. Satisfaction Guaranteed

Published by Brewers Publications

Notes

Notes

Notes

Notes

Notes